HOCKEY 76

**Action during the quarter final of the Major Junior A playoffs between Toronto
Marlies and the Kingston Canadians.**

**Right: A winning shot in the match
between Toronto Maple Leafs and the Minnesota
North Stars on March 8th, this year.**

Overleaf: Bobby Orr.

HOCKEY 76

Brian McFarlane

Two Continents, New York · Methuen, Toronto

Published in the United States
by Two Continents/Methuen Publications
30 East 42 St. New York 10017

Published in Canada
by Methuen Publications
2330 Midland Avenue
Agincourt, Ontario

ISBN Canada 0 458 91340 5

ISBN U.S.A. 0 8467 0102 2

Library of Congress
Catalog Card Number 75-13916

Printed and Bound in Canada

1 2 3 4 5 6   0 9 8 7 6 5

Contents ⤳

Credits

Paul Bereswill, 94
Peter Connal, 12 (below)
Bill Galloway, 142, 143 (below)
Harvard Sports News Bureau, 44, 46 (above)
Ray Jubinville, 47, 78 (below)
Dennis Miles, 1, 8, 74
Bernie Moser, Dufor Photographers, 32
Public Archives of Canada, 44 (above)
Scotiabank Hockey College, 92, 95, 149, 158
Robert B. Shaver, 12 (above), 58, 81, (above), 84 (below), 93
    110, 132, 144, 145, 146, 147, 148, 150, 152, 153 (above), 154
David Simpson, 15, 16, 17, 19, 24, 27, 66, 71
Toronto Star Syndicate, 88
Toronto Sun Photo, 2, 3, 77

Acknowledgements

The author and publishers wish to thank the following for permission to use articles published in this volume

THE CHICAGO TRIBUNE MAGAZINE
"Keeping Peace Among the Pros" and "Hockey Mania", from the January 19, 1975 edition

COOPER CANADA LIMITED
"Hockey Coaches Clinic Power Skating Drills"

LESLIE McFARLANE
"Playoff Warrior"

ONIL MERCIER
From Trees to Hat Tricks

BILL REID
Pee Wee cartoons from Scotiabank Hockey News

SCOTIABANK HOCKEY COLLEGE
"Thousands of Young Canadians Flock to Unique Hockey College"
"Santa Skates and Scores"
"Any Old Patch of Ice Will Do"

Guy Lafleur

On the night of April 5, 1975, the Montreal Canadiens beat the luckless Washington Capitals 10-2 in Montreal's second to last game of the regular season. Guy Lafleur scored his 53rd goal of the season at 15:53 of the first period. Lafleur established the mark for most goals in a season for a right winger, a record previously held by Mickey Redmond.

The matter-of-fact report of the Washington game says next to nothing about Guy Lafleur who, after four years in a Montreal hockey uniform, has finally blossomed into the scoring role everyone predicted of him when he graduated from junior hockey. Three years ago a lot of people would never have believed that Lafleur could score as he did last season; two years ago his coaches were asking themselves whether he could cut it in the pros. 1975 proved that Lafleur could do it.

Four years ago Guy Lafleur came to the Canadiens from the Quebec Ramparts, a junior team in Quebec City, where Lafleur had done practically everything that it was possible for a forward to do. In 218 games at Quebec he had scored 314 goals, 130 of them in his final year. The Canadiens were looking for someone to replace the retired Jean Beliveau and the bilingual Lafleur fit right into their plans. But California Golden Seals had first pick in the junior draft, and it was only through some complicated deals by Montreal, which included sending Ralph Backstrom to the Los Angeles Kings, that allowed Montreal to have California's first amateur pick, giving them the opportunity to pick up Lafleur.

Guy's first three seasons were more of a nightmare than a dream of playing in the NHL. A great deal was expected of him, and the pressure was tremendous. It's true that he scored 29, 28, and 21 goals for a total of 78 in those first three years. But when fans recalled his 130 goals in his final junior season, the NHL totals looked very weak indeed, especially since other shooters such as Phil Esposito of the Bruins were collecting 50 plus goals a season on a regular basis.

"The first three years weren't easy," Lafleur recalls. "I was always nervous, before the games, during the games, after the games. I was worried that people would think I wasn't working and that they would compare me with Beliveau and (Henri) Richard. I was worried all the time."

But Lafleur learned to relax, stopped listening to his tormentors and began to play his own game. Coach Scotty Bowman of the Canadiens gave him lots of ice time and showed that he still had confidence in Lafleur. Jean Beliveau helped. And, after his third season, Lafleur was becoming more content with his own play, even though his totals on that season, 21 goals and 35 assists, were not impressive.

"I was pleased with my third season," Lafleur says. "I did not get as many points as I might have, but I was getting the chances."

And the chances turned to goals in the 1974-75 campaign. At the Jean Beliveau golf tournament prior to this season, Lafleur was overheard saying that he was going to show his detractors that he could play hockey, and show them he did. He reported to training camp fit as a fiddle, and when the exhibition season began he cast his helmet aside along with the "yellow" tag that had been whispered about him from rink to rink. He took the checks and built up his confidence on the ice. He worked hard, never stopped skating either in games or in practices. He improved his back checking and stickhandling.

Even though he looked good in training camp and the exhibition games, the regular season started out like so many others before. It was eight games before he netted his first goal, but from there on in, everything went Lafleur's way. By mid-season Lafleur had 32 goals, second highest in the league and more than his previous entire season high of 29. His 35 assists placed him third in the scoring race.

In February, Guy suffered a setback when he was slashed by Darryl Sittler in Toronto and broke a finger in his left hand. At this time he had 44 goals and 52 assists for 96 points, tying the Canadien team record set in 1958 by Dickie Moore and equalled by Frank Mahovlich. When he returned to the team, Lafleur picked up right where he had left off.

Guy Lafleur has become a hero in Montreal. He is becoming another Beliveau in the eyes not only of Montreal fans, but of fans across the country. This is the new-look Guy Lafleur, with a vision of finishing his career with a record similar to other Montreal greats like Maurice Richard and Jean Beliveau. Guy Lafleur might do even better than that.

Young hockey players are often quite full of themselves. While playing junior A hockey in Windsor one night, I skated in alone on the Windsor goaltender. I gave him a deke, flipped the puck high . . . and scored. Back on the bench, I told my teammates "That goalie . . . whoever he is . . . isn't so hot."

Later, I learned the goalie's name . . . Glenn Hall. Hall went on to a brilliant career in the NHL. As for me . . . that goal was the only one I ever scored against him.

Two Toronto Maple Leaf players who suffered through a dismal playoff series were goalie Doug Favell and defenseman Jim McKenny. Favell didn't play a single game and McKenny was roundly booed by Toronto fans.

After the final game, Favell quipped: "Now we're both going south to share a nervous breakdown." And McKenny, told he hadn't made a single mistake in the final game, deadpanned: "Gee, I must have had an off-night."

10

Is Hockey Too Violent?

William McMurtry thinks pro hockey is too violent. He objects to slow-motion replays of hockey fights and he doesn't think too highly of Peter Puck, either.

"Hockey is the Canadian common denominator," he says. "But it must be reformed. Hockey need not be a symptom of a sick society."

Those opinions were voiced several months ago when McMurtry, a Toronto lawyer commissioned by the Ontario government to investigate violence in amateur hockey, lashed out at the professionals.

"The professionals, notably in the National Hockey League," he judged, "are the unfortunate models for most of the amateur players. Hockey is the only sport where physical intimidation outside the rules is encouraged as a legitimate tactic, leading to the glorification of the brawlers in an attempt to sell the game to U.S. audiences.

"It is time the real hockey fans insisted that the players be allowed to play hockey.

"The way the rules are enforced, a player has no reason for turning his back and refusing to fight," he said.

"In fact, if a player refuses to fight, and an opponent for no particular reason deliberately punches him, and even knocks him senseless, the appropriate penalty at the present time is a two minute penalty.

"With rules such as this is it any wonder that we have seen the emergence of the Broad Street Bullies?"

Mention of the Broad Street Bullies brought a quick counter-attack from their leader, coach Fred Shero.

Shero, defending the Philadelphia Flyers' strongarm tactics, said McMurtry was not competent to criticize hockey.

"The National Hockey League," he said, "can police its own game. It needs no help from outside . . . from lawyers like McMurtry.

"Why is everybody up in arms over violence in hockey? Look at football. Players die like flies in football. There's over 20 deaths a year in that sport."

Shero said he opposes any rule changes to restrict the body contact prevalent in the NHL. He said hockey is a comparatively safe sport and that the number of penalties his Philadelphia team receives (a record 1,969 minutes in 1974-75) is ample proof of the league's attempt to keep the game in order.

NHL president Clarence Campbell dismissed McMurtry's report as a product of the commissioner's imagination.

"I don't accept his summations at all," said Campbell. "A great deal of that report is a product of his (McMurtry's) personal assessment for which he has neither the mandate nor the competence. It's a product of his imagination."

Campbell has often maintained that fights in hockey serve as a "safety valve" and that hockey fights seldom result in injury beyond scrapes and bruises.

Many hockey men agree. "Take the fighting out of hockey," said one OHA executive, "and the players will resort to butt ending and spearing each other with their sticks. Those are far more serious infractions than fighting."

McMurtry rebutted the argument with this comment, "That's like claiming that if society punishes shoplifters they will automatically become bank robbers."

Fighting is part of the game. Tempers flare often in hockey, but seldom do the pugilists get hurt.

This brawl at the Montreal Forum between the Habs and the Flyers involved all players from both teams.

Alan Eagleson, president of the National Hockey League Player's Association (and a law partner of McMurtry's) said the overwhelming reaction of players was, "Oh, here we go again" when McMurtry's 47-page report was issued.

"There's a great deal of difference between professional hockey and amateur hockey," stated Eagleson. "In amateur hockey there's no reason for violence. In pro hockey, a player takes certain risks. There's nothing wrong with Bill's report as it applies to amateur hockey, but the fans will dictate what changes are necessary in pro hockey.''

King Clancy and other oldtimers who have been around the pro game since the NHL was formed in 1917 generally agree that hockey is a lot *less* violent today that it was decades ago.

Many of McMurtry's proposals, however, were quite acceptable . . . even to the pros.

"It must be established," he stated, "that there is a purpose to amateur hockey other than that of training professionals, since statistics show that less than 1 per cent of the boys playing in organized hockey will ever turn professional.

"The standard of referees should also be upgraded and efforts made to educate fans and parents in the purposes and objectives of amateur hockey.''

Parents too came in for sharp criticism for their sometimes hysterical demands for victory at any price while seldom realizing the extent of the cost.

McMurtry struck a bullseye when he said, "The obsessive influence and involvement of the adults may in the long run destroy the most essential ingredient of all in developing hockey skill . . . sheer love of the game.''

McMurtry suggested that the government help by providing more money for the sport and back the establishment of a powerful hockey council. He also suggested a revival of school-oriented hockey programs (similar to those in the U.S.) involving as many players as possible.

"It surprises me," he said, "to discover we have sufficient funds for swimming pools but not enough to build rinks for school children.''

McMurtry attacked television coverage of hockey games but stopped short of censorship.

He wants the television industry to "de-emphasize those aspects of the pro game that are undesirable as an example to our youth.''

He writes: "It is worth noting that the coverage in professional football seems to emphasize far more the finesse of the game, and this in a game that has more that its share of violence.''

Hockey broadcasters, he suggests, should not unduly exploit a particularly violent incident by showing it three times.

Even Peter Puck came in for a share of the criticism. The much-heralded animated cartoon series designed to explain hockey rules, regulations and intricacies met McMurtry's disapproval because "the players were characterized as brutal top heavy Neanderthal types who were shown demonstrating every type of foul with great gusto and relish.''

McMurtry may not like Peter and his pals, but the TV ratings and the mail response indicate that most fans do . . . especially the young fans. And not one response in a thousand mentions anything about brutality or violence.

McMurtry wins almost universal agreement with his conclusion.

"Hockey can be an effective instrument to improve the social conditions. Hockey can be a positive educational force, a model, to instill values such as co-operation, personal discipline, tolerance and understanding . . . a celebration of speed, courage and finesse.

"Rather than a divisive force, fuelled by calculated animosities, it can and should be a bond between participants, with a shared commitment to excellence and the common love of the game, hockey, which perhaps more than any other can give one a sense of physical exhilaration and sheer joy of participation.''

DAWSON CITY DAREDEVILS

BY BRIAN McFARLANE

"Hey, Gramps, tell us a hockey story, willyu?"

"Yeah, come on, Gramps. Tell us about the time you played against King Clancy and punched him in the nose."

The voices came from the top of the stairs. They belonged to Allan and Bruce, twin grandsons of the man who'd punched Clancy in the nose.

Grandpa Wilson pushed aside the paper he'd been reading after dinner and winked at his daughter Joan. "Those boys of yours," he said. "Is that all they think about these days — hockey?"

Joan laughed. "They come by it honestly, Dad. Seems that's all I ever heard around our house when I was growing up. When you weren't playing the game you were talking about it and when you weren't talking about it you were reading about it or listening to it on the radio. Now, whenever you visit, the kids think you're a regular expert. And what's this about punching King Clancy in the nose?"

"Ah, it's just a little story I told the boys last time I was here. More a shove than a punch. King and I played against each other a long time ago. Anyway, I guess I can tell them a story before they go to sleep.

"Come down here, boys!" he shouted.

The boys, fresh from their bath and ready for bed, came scuttling down the stairs. Allan was wearing hockey gloves and Bruce had discarded his normal pajama top in favor of a Boston Bruins' jersey with a big number 4 on the back. They were Christmas gifts, from grandpa of course. The boys bounced up on the sofa and settled in beside their favorite visitor.

"Make it a short story," admonished Joan. "It's way past their bedtime already."

"All right, a short story it is . . . about the longest journey ever taken by a gang of hockey players who wanted to win the Stanley Cup."

Alan looked up quizzically. "Is this a true story, Gramps?" he asked.

"Of course it's true, my father told this story to me, many times, when I was just about your age. He was there when this story happened in Ottawa a great many years ago. He saw the very games I'm going to tell you about. Now, shall I go on, or . . . "

"Oh yes, go on Gramps. You tell great hockey stories," Allan urged, punching his new Christmas gloves together.

"All right, then," said Gramps, waggling a finger for silence. "If there's no more interruptions I'll tell you all about the team from the Klondike that challenged for the Stanley Cup. It was the most remarkable challenge in the history of the Cup. And it took place way back in 1905.

14

"In those days, the Stanley Cup was just a small silver bowl, about the size of a football. And almost any team could challenge for it. This was long before anybody even thought of starting up the NHL.

"In Ottawa, where I was born, all the young fellows played hockey. My dad was a fine player and I remember the times he'd take me along with him and we'd play shinny on the Rideau Canal. But my dad wasn't nearly good enough to play for the best team in Ottawa. The team there was called the Silver Seven. At first there were only seven of them. They didn't have a lot of subs on a team in those days. And they got their name when their manager, a fellow by the name of Shillington, presented each of the players who joined his club with a silver nugget.

"It was in 1903 when the Silver Seven started playing some of the roughest, toughest, most sensational hockey ever seen. They had a fellow named Frank McGee, and he was the greatest scorer of his day. He was big and blond but he had a handicap. McGee had trouble seeing out of one eye. His vision was partly blurred, but if it bothered him on the hockey rink he never said so. And later, he was able to serve in World War I with the Canadian army. Just the same, they called him "One-Eyed" Frank McGee and he played the hero's role in this story I'm telling you.

"On the Silver Seven there was an all-round athlete, Harvey Pulford, who'd nail you with a bodycheck and never look back to see if you were dead or alive. There were the Gilmour brothers ... if you fought one you'd better be ready to fight them all. Their names were Dave, Suddie and Bill. Three of 'em. And the two Smith brothers, Harry and Alf. Harry (Rat) Westwick, only 135 pounds and don't ask me how he got his nickname 'cause I don't know. Bouse Hutton and Percy Lesueur played goal for that team. Lesueur used the same goal stick in every game, league and

15

playoffs, for five straight years, and right now that stick is down in the Hockey Hall of Fame. Those are some of the names I remember . . . some of the stars my dad told me about. A few played a year or two then moved on. But mostly, as I say, there were only seven on the team at one time. The Silver Seven!"

"Were they big and tough, Gramps. Like the Philadelphia Flyers?" asked Allan, catching the start of a yawn in his hockey glove.

"Tough! I'll say they were tough. When they played Toronto one year they hit the Toronto players on the hands and arms so hard they could barely control the puck. And when Toronto complained about it, one Ottawa player said, 'Gee, Toronto get off easy. When we played Winnipeg last year, most of their players got carried off on stretchers.'

"So those were the Silver Seven. And one year, they received the strangest

challenge in all of Stanley Cup history. Away up in the Yukon, thousands of miles away, a bunch of fellows had formed a hockey team in Dawson City. They were a ragged band of players . . . most of them lured to the Yukon by the sight of gold. At the turn of the century thousands of men rushed to the Klondike hoping to strike it rich. They were brash, strong, adventurous young men — real daredevils — and when they weren't panning the streams and rivers or digging in the hills for gold, they played hockey.

"There was a goalie from Three Rivers . . . so young he barely shaved. His name was Albert Forrest and he was 17 years old. On defense — or as they called it in those days, point and cover point — they had Jim Johnstone from Ottawa and Dr. Randy McLennan from Cornwall. The right winger, Norm Watt, came from Aylmer, Quebec, and the left winger, George Kennedy, was from somewhere in Manitoba. So was the centerman, Hec

16

Smith, and a player they called the rover who was Dave Fairbairn. The Dawson City team had one spare, A.N. Martin from Ottawa.

"Of course, nobody in the East had ever heard of these fellows until the Silver Seven received a challenge from the Dawson City lads. Imagine a team from the Klondike dreaming they could steal the Stanley Cup away from the greatest hockey team in the world!

"At first the Ottawa players just laughed. They scoffed at the idea of playing a band of second-raters. But some of them admitted the idea of meeting a team from the Yukon was appealing. Maybe they thought the upstarts might bring some gold along and spread it around. Anyway, they accepted the challenge.

"Now there were no fancy jet planes in those days. There was no fast way to get from Dawson City to Ottawa. How the Dawson City players made the trip to Canada's capital city is a story in itself.

First, they needed money. So they talked a rich old prospector, Colonel Joe Boyle, into bankrolling the expedition. The Colonel was a good sport. He knew the Klondikers weren't very good but he put up some money and the journey was on.

"On the afternoon of December 19, 1904, the boys left Dawson City. And they went by dog team! Practically the whole town turned out to see them off and wish them luck. That first day they covered less than 50 miles. They didn't do nearly so well on the second. And by the third day they were suffering from blistered feet so they covered only 35 miles. All this time it was bitter cold . . . nearly 20 degrees below zero. Their destination was Skagway, on the Alaska coast, where they planned to make boat connections to Seattle. They arrived in Skagway, half frozen and exhausted, only to discover the boat had left without them! They'd missed connections by a mere two hours!

"Well, some friendly townsfolk took them in, fed and bathed them, and made the team relax until the next boat came in. That turned out to be five days later.

"Their boat finally arrived and they clambered aboard, eager to get moving again, to continue their quest for the Stanley Cup. It was a rough ride to Seattle and some of the boys were seasick but they finally arrived and stepped ashore. Then it was up to Vancouver by train, over the border and back into Canada. Imagine what the border men must have thought when the players were asked where they were going in Canada and why.

"'We're going to Ottawa' they said.

"'We're going to play a couple of hockey games there and we're going to bring back the Stanley Cup.'

"From Vancouver the Dawson City boys headed East by train and they were astonished to learn they had become rather famous. The story of their trip was written up in the papers, and at various stops along the way, people came out to the stations to meet them. Hockey fans shook them by the hand and wished them luck against the Silver Seven.

"With this kind of fan support to cheer them, they arrived in Ottawa on Jan. 12, 1905, almost a full month after beginning their 4,000 mile jaunt. They were dreadfully tired and since they hadn't had a chance to practice, they asked the Silver Seven for a week's postponement of the two-game series. Naturally Ottawa refused. Why take chances? And besides, they had more important games to play. No, a postponement was out of the question.

"The arrogance of the Silver Seven must have annoyed the Dawson City boys. And one of them, Norm Watt, turned out to be the bad man in the first game of the series. He spent 15 minutes in the penalty box after he hit Ottawa's Art Moore over the head with his stick. Later he tangled with Alf Smith and was sent off for another 10 minutes. Meanwhile, the Silver Seven were pouring in

the goals. Poor Albert Forrest, the 17-year-old goalie! He never had a chance as the Silver Seven romped to a 9-2 victory. The Dawson City players were disconsolate. To come all this way to take such a drubbing.

"But there was one small consolation. The Dawson City players had held the legendary Frank McGee to a single goal. And they had started to get their ice legs back in the second half. Maybe game two would be a different story.

"There was a famous tavern in Ottawa where many of the sportsmen of the era gathered to talk sport and make friendly wagers. Not the sort of place I'd ever want to see you fellows in. But the Dawson City boys soon found it and began sampling the refreshments. Naturally, they took a ribbing from the local sports fans about the first-game loss. One Ottawa supporter called over to the Dawson City table, 'I'll bet you've never laid eyes on a player the likes of Frank McGee. Ain't he the greatest scorer in the whole darn world?'

"One Dawson City forward rose to the bait. 'Ah, McGee's not so hot,' he answered. 'He didn't impress me too much.'

"'I'll tell him you said so,' the local fan cackled. 'Maybe old Frank will show you a trick or two you've never seen before when you meet up with him again.'

"And Frank must have got the message because what he did to the poor Klondikers in the second game, well, it's almost unbelievable.

"There were two halves or periods in those days, not three like in hockey today. And Frank didn't waste any time getting started. He took the puck and scored four goals in a flash. Holding him back must have been like holding back one of those rushing rivers they have up in the Klondike. But it was in the second half that McGee *really* went to work. He scored 10 more times against a dazed Albert Forrest. And records McGee set in that game stand to this day. I doubt if they'll ever be broken! He scored eight

18

consecutive goals in a span of eight minutes and 20 seconds. Three of those goals in a minute and a half and four of them in 140 seconds. What a fantastic display of scoring he put on! And don't forget he could barely see out of one eye.

"Well, the final score was 23-2 for the Silver Seven. The only thing big league about the Dawson City players was their uniforms. They cut fancy figures in black, white and gold outfits and one or two of them looked like they knew what the game was all about.

"And boys, even though they lost, they helped contribute an exciting chapter to the hockey history book. And you know something else, they were also responsible for the first big rush on hockey tickets. People were so intrigued with their bold bid to win the Cup that crowds stormed the old Dey's Arena in Ottawa hoping to see them play. Your great grandfather was one of the lucky ones because Frank McGee helped get him in.

"So the team that journeyed the farthest, and suffered the most hardship along the way, was also the team that absorbed the worst beating, the most humiliating defeat in the history of Stanley Cup play."

With that Grandpa gave a great big yawn and looked at the twin boys; they were both fast asleep.

Goalie Brophy of Montreal Westmount made hockey history in 1905 when he rushed down the ice and slapped the puck past a stunned Paddy Moran in the Quebec nets. Brophy repeated the feat the following season.

In a game between Rat Portage and Ottawa in 1905, the referee wore a hard hat to protect himself from fans and players alike. In the same game, Rat Portage claimed that Ottawa had salted the ice to slow down the visitors.

Thousands Flock to Unique "Hockey College"

For the past six years, I've been closely associated with a unique hockey college. This hockey college has no campus, no classrooms, no tuition fees, no professors and (hurray!) no homework.

I'm talking about the Scotiabank Hockey College, which embraces over 140,000 young Canadians from coast-to-coast through over 1,000 branches of the Bank of Nova Scotia. And it's growing all the time.

In fact, I'm looking forward to the day when our first hockey playing Scotiabank Hockey College member makes the NHL or WHA. Surely, one or two of our earliest members will soon be ready for big league stardom.

What is my role with the Scotiabank Hockey College? Well, they call me the

The Hockey College Directors, Beliveau, McFarlane and Howe.

Dean of the Hockey College. Pretty fancy title, right? And my job is to supervise Hockey College activities as well as write and edit a monthly hockey news bulletin which goes to Hockey College members.

Shortly after the Hockey College was introduced, Jean Beliveau and Gordie Howe were named Hockey College Directors. What a thrill it was for me to become associated with these two hockey giants! It was almost as though someone had asked me to play on the same hockey line with them.

Let me explain how and why young hockey fans join the Scotiabank Hockey College.

First of all, membership is free.

Membership is achieved simply by opening a small savings account in any branch of the Bank of Nova Scotia, anywhere in Canada. Any youngster who opens an account for as little as $1.00 will automatically become a Hockey College member. He (or she) then receives a Hockey College decal and is entitled to receive an exclusive copy of the Hockey College News. This is a monthly bulletin filled with hockey articles, tips on how to play hockey, plus a centerfold photograph (in color) of a star player. Members are encouraged to pick up a copy of the Hockey College News when they make regular monthly deposits in their savings accounts.

Sherry Clayton co-ordinates all Hockey College activities from the Toronto headquarters.

Regular deposits are important because they keep members eligible for major prizes in a special lucky draw conducted each month. Twelve times a year, 25 lucky draw winners receive bicycles, skates, watches, and if they're really lucky, an all-expense paid trip for two to a big league hockey game. At least once a year, the Hockey College holds an extra special lucky draw and the winner here gets an all expense paid trip to Disney World in Florida.

I've been pleased with the reaction of

Faye Acton types up information from application cards on a keyplex machine.

A copy of the news as it comes off the press.

hockey men to the Hockey College concept. Several of the top players I've talked to said they wished there'd been a similar program for them when they were younger. They also like the idea of girls becoming members. Approximately thirty per cent of the Hockey College members at the moment are girls.

Clarence Campbell, President of the NHL, once told me he was completely in accord with any plan that encouraged thrift and proper savings habits among the young. If it tied in with hockey, so much the better.

Because the money invested in each member's account earns interest at the highest savings account rate, I like to think many young Canadians will consider their Hockey College account as a university education savings plan. Supervisor of all Hockey College activities at the Bank of Nova Scotia's Head Office in Toronto is Mrs. Sherry Clayton.

"Being involved with hockey and young people, not to mention great hockey men like Howe and Beliveau, is really exciting," says Mrs. Clayton.

21

Another Pee Wee cartoon comes to life.

Elsie Farwell and Rosemary Anderson chat with Faye. Together they are responsible for ensuring that you are recorded as an official member.

"And it's always a pleasure to inform some member he's won a major prize like a trip to an NHL game or a trip to Disney World."

A full time columnist for the Hockey College News is Montreal's Barry Blitt. Barry has been writing for the Hockey College News for over three years now.

A favorite with readers of the News is cartoonist Bill Reid, who draws the comic strip Pee Wee and his Pals. Bill says he knew when he was just six years old that he was going to be a cartoonist. Pee Wee also appears throughout this book.

In my travels, I'm always pleased when a youngster comes up to me and says, "Hi, Mr. McFarlane. I'm a member of the Hockey College." I'm even more pleased when one of them says he won a trip to an NHL game or a pair of skates or some other prize.

And I can't wait for the day, when just before I interview a rookie star in the NHL, he'll turn to me and say, "Hey, I know you're waiting for one of the Hockey College members to play in the NHL. Well, I guess I'm your man."

Jean Beliveau meet two young members.

PHOTO QUIZ

Recognize these hockey players? We'll give you one or two clues, then you're on your own. Answers are at the back of the book.

1. Plays with his father and brother.

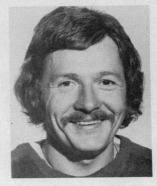

2. Red Wing goalie

3. Islander rearguard.

4. Detroit's Danny boy.

5. North Star puck stopper.

6. Frequently wears a head band.

PLAYOFF WARRIOR

BY LESLIE McFARLANE

Picking up the puck inside the blue line, "Duke" Blake went back behind the net, came around, and skated up the middle, pushing the rubber ahead of him.

Out of the corners of his shrewd eyes, he glanced right and left without turning his head. His wings were with him; the Flyer forwards were waiting. McMunn, the opposing center, was skating slowly backward at a half crouch, his stick extended, ready for a poke or sweep check.

Duke Blake swung sharply to the right then back to the left, and finally broke straight ahead. But the moves weren't quick enough. He failed to pull McMunn out of position. The other man's stick lashed out quickly and knocked the puck spinning. In the same instant, McMunn hurdled Blake's stick, snapped up the puck, and broke fast for the goal.

A great roar went up from the crowd! McMunn's wings tried to break with him and were struggling with their checks along the boards. Duke Blake swung around and gave chase, but before he had taken three strides, McMunn was swooping in on the Mohawk's defense and had his shot away.

The goalie slid across the net, took it on his pads and cleared to the corner. Old-time hockey fans in the crowd looked at one another and shook their heads. It was a Flyer crowd, Duke Blake was playing for the visiting team, but the fans still regarded him as one of their own.

Duke Blake had played with the Flyers for years. One of the greatest players of the game, he had given the Flyers his best, season after season. And now, he was back there in front of the old home crowd, playing in a rival uniform.

Duke Blake, in the sunset of his great hockey career, had been traded to the Mohawks! Followers of the Flyer team shook their heads. In the old days, when Duke Blake was at his peak, a Duke Blake rush down the ice was something to send a jolt through thousands of watchers; something to bring a mob to its feet in a howling frenzy; something to leave them tingling and weak with excitement.

You had never really seen perfection in skating and stick-handling unless you had seen Duke on an end-to-end rush in the old days when he was a star!

But those days were gone. Now, here was the old Duke, in a strange uniform, going through the motions of those dazzling rushes of past years — but just the motions. The old speed and dash were gone. The Duke was on the way out.

Smith, the Mohawk left defense, went into the corner for the puck and drifted it up to the blue line, where Keeley, left-winger, picked it up. Keeley clashed with his check and they fought it out along the boards. Duke Blake grabbed the loose puck and broke with it.

McMunn closed in on him. Duke dodged and shifted, but McMunn was right at his heels, pestering him, harrying him. There was a time when Duke would have toyed with McMunn or any other rookie center, would have handcuffed him, made a monkey out of him and broken like lightning into one of his zigzag swooping rushes.

But the old explosive spark was missing. Duke fumbled and lost the puck. But McMunn had plenty of respect for the veteran. Even if he was on the way out, you didn't fool with the hockeywise Duke. McMunn laid a quick pass over to his right wing and the fight went on.

Hansen, the dour, sharp-featured coach of the Mohawks, sent out his top line at the next off-side.

Duke skated slowly over. Some of his old fans gave him a hand, but it was merely like a rustling of dry leaves in the wind compared to the storm of clapping that used to surge from one end of the rink to the other whenever Duke skated to the bench.

Duke sat down heavily. He glanced up along the blue seats to a certain section, a certain row. A thin, bright-faced boy of fourteen waved to him encouragingly. Duke winked.

"My kid brother," he explained gruffly to Keeley, who was sitting beside him and had noticed the silent interchange. "Never misses a game."

"Going to be a hockey player?" asked Keeley.

Duke shook his head. His eyes were somber. "Crippled," he said briefly. "He's got a bad foot."

"Tough," mumbled Keeley.

"Yeah, it's tough."

Duke watched the game. The Mohawks were cutting loose with a fast, sustained attack that was clicking on all cylinders. They were swarming around

the Flyer net.

Duke knew there wasn't any sentiment in hockey. He had given the best years of his career to the Flyers, but he knew now that he couldn't expect gratitude. Hockey was a business, he knew that. But there had been something particularly callous and hardboiled in the way Al Metzer, the Flyer manager, had let him go to the Mohawks without a word of regret. The deal had been completed secretly, and Duke had been one of the last to hear about it.

Surely — after giving the Flyers his best for twelve years, keeping them on top, helping them win four championships, making them a drawing card on the road and making money for Metzer and his stockholders — surely he had deserved better treatment than to be sold cheaply to the Mohawks like any two-bit player.

The Flyers were cooped up. There was a crash, as two husky players went down against the boards. The puck skimmed into the open. One of the Flyers lifted it down the ice. Players whirled, darting after it.

"Boy, I'd like to see us take those guys tonight!" grunted Duke.

He was an old man as hockey players go, and yet he was still on the sunny side of forty, with thick, black hair, close-set, shrewd blue eyes, thin, firm mouth and a strong jaw.

It was odd for him to be sitting there on the visitor's bench, watching the Flyers and hoping they would be licked, hoping that big crowd of Flyer fans would be sent home disappointed.

"They gave you a raw deal, all right," said Keeley.

"Raw deal!" growled Duke. "I'll tell the world. I hope they finish in the cellar!"

"Hey Blake. That guy McMunn is making you look like a monkey out there tonight," snapped the harsh voice of Hansen, the Mohawk coach.

Duke looked at him. He had never liked Hansen. He was one of the slave-driving types, a tough, hard-bitten fellow with a sharp tongue, sparse with praise, but free with abuse.

Duke Blake didn't answer.

"You heard me," rasped the coach irritably.

"Sure I heard you."

"Well, then, do something about it next time I send you out there! Earn your pay! This isn't an Old Folk's Home, you know."

Duke reddened. Some of the fans in back of the bench heard that crack. The other players on the bench heard it too. Hansen meant that they should. But they pretended not to notice.

Duke was sore. Next time Hansen sent the line out, Duke faced McMunn grimly, his mouth twisted in an ugly line. So this was what you had to take when you began to slow up a little! Discarded by a money-grubber like Metzer, bawled out by a rat like Hansen.

Clack! Sticks smacked together. Duke snagged the rubber from McMunn, broke away from the rival center, and flew down the ice.

Duke swung in on the defense. A Flyer wing got into the clear and tried to check him, but Duke stickhandled his way past and left the other player fanning the ice.

Slowing up, maybe, but he still had a few old tricks up his sleeve.

McMunn swept alongside, hacking at Duke's stick, trying to throw him off stride. Duke flipped an easy, deceptive shot toward the goal. The puck bounced and rolled.

Players were milling all around him. Duke side-stepped a defense man. The goalie came out and took a slap at the skittering puck, but it bounced crazily away from his stick.

A Mohawk wing and his check went blundering into the goalie, and all three went down in a heap. Duke had his eye fixed on that black bit of rubber now resting on the ice almost on the line — with the net gaping wide open.

He lunged for it. But McMunn's stick was pressed firmly on his own. McMunn was shoving him out of the play. Duke couldn't get his stick clear; couldn't get it free to shove that puck across the line.

Duke burned with a bitter desire to beat the Flyers, to get revenge on the team that had discarded him, to show Hansen he still had plenty of hockey in his system. He wrenched back his stick.

McMunn struck swiftly, batted the loose puck past the goalpost and into the corner. Duke saw his chance slipping. He struck, hooked McMunn's skates out from under him. The center

27

went down with a crash. There was still a chance to get that puck.

The whistle was shrilling, the crowd roaring. Duke looked up and saw the referee thumbing him to the penalty box.

Duke Blake shrugged and skated slowly over to the gate. Many in the crowd were silent. They didn't like to see Duke taking penalties. In the old days, he had been one of the cleanest players in the league. But a lot of the fans hadn't seen Duke in the old days. They jeered him derisively now.

Duke Blake being jeered by a Flyer crowd! That was one for the book.

With the odd-man advantage, the Flyers turned on the heat. They launched a vicious attack, ripped open the Mohawk defense, and tore through for a smart goal on a triple pass. It was the third period, and this was the first goal of the game.

They faced-off and attacked again. An accidental trip sent another Mohawk forward to the penalty box, and the game blew up. The Flyers rammed in another goal.

When Duke skated out he was immediately called to the bench. Hansen glared at him.

"I suppose you know you've cost us this game!" rapped the coach.

"With a little luck, I'd have won it."

"You need all your luck. You haven't got anything else," barked Hansen.

Toward the end of the period, Hansen said to Cariff, a utility man: "See what you can do at center." And to Duke Blake: "You'd better stay in and rest. You look tired." Hansen's voice was acid.

Duke went white. There were only a few minutes to go, and the game was lost. Hansen was benching him out of sheer spite, out of nothing more than a desire to humiliate him in front of the crowd that had once shrieked his praises, in the very rink where he had won his greatest fame.

He rested his arms on the boards and watched the shifting figures out there on the ice. His face was impassive. He could hear a fan up in the row back of the box:

"Did you get that? They've benched Duke!"

Duke Blake's mouth twisted bitterly. What a game! Give it your best, give it your life, and what does it give you? Some money, sure, and applause when you're going good, then jeers and the gate when you begin to slip. It was a mean, rotten, soulless racket.

"Hockey!" he whispered bitterly, scornfully, from between clenched teeth.

Duke Blake had hot words with Hansen in the dressing room after the game. Ike Starrett, the manager, got into the argument, too. Hansen and Starrett were two of a kind, unpopular in the league and unpopular with their own players.

"Lose a game for us and then want to know why you're benched!" snorted Starrett. "I told Hansen to bench you. So what?"

"In any other city I wouldn't mind so much —"

"Don't like being shown up in front of your old home crowd, huh?" said Hansen. "Well, we didn't do it. You showed yourself up. You were terrible tonight, Blake, and if you don't snap out of it pretty soon, we won't ask you to dress for any more games. Maybe they could use you on the Panthers."

The Panther outfit was the Mohawk club's minor league farm team.

"I'll hang up my skates before I'll play for the Panthers," snapped Duke.

Duke strode out of the dressing room. They were catching a midnight flight and he did not have much time for a talk with his kid brother, Alex. The youngster was waiting for him in the corridor.

"Come on kid," said Duke. "We'll have time for a coffee."

He had spent the day with Alex and his mother. Since being sold to the Mohawks, Duke had seen little of his family—a few hours whenever the team had a game with the Flyers, and that was all.

"That was pretty rotten of Hansen, dropping you in the last period," said Alex loyally, as he limped along beside Duke. "He just did it out of spite. You played all right Duke. It wasn't your fault they lost. With any luck at all, you'd have scored."

"It's the old legs, Alex," explained Duke. "They go first. A hockey player or a fighter or a ball-player — he's only as good as his legs. But that doesn't mean he's all washed up when he begins to lose a little speed. I'm not as fast as I was . . ."

"You looked pretty fast out there to-night, Duke."

"I'm still a lot faster than some guys. And I've still got my hockey brains. What beats me is the way the crowd rides a fellow just because he isn't as good as he was five years ago. The minute you begin to slip, seems to me they all want to give you another shove on the toboggan. Turn in one bad game, and they forget all the good games you ever played."

"Don't worry about them, Duke. You're the best player that ever stepped on the ice, and they can't take that away from you."

Duke grinned, "You're all wet, kid, but it's nice to have you think so. I knew I had one good fan rooting for me to-night anyway."

"More than me, Duke. Most of that crowd was pulling for you. Maybe there were some who never saw you play when . . . well, when you were with the Flyers, but you shouldn't worry."

There was a warm feeling in Duke's heart when he boarded the plane that night after putting Alex in a taxi.

"I have one loyal fan anyhow," he said to himself.

The Mohawks dropped two home games. Duke Blake suited up but didn't play with the team on their next road trip. This was a direct slap in Duke's face. It caused a stir in the hockey world.

Duke took it silently. He had nothing to say when reporters tried to draw him out. Inwardly, he was boiling. His temper was not improved by a sports columnist's comment:

Looks as if Duke Blake, one of the great hockey players, is definitely on the way out. Duke has had a poor season and has been a big disappointment to the Mohawk management.

Duke has been slowing up for several seasons, and all those who recall his spectacular play when he was at his peak will regret that he did not hang up his skates at the end of last season and retire gracefully from the game.

Being benched from the Mohawk line-up when the team went on the road is a humiliation, and Duke isn't adding to his reputation by sticking around. It is generally known that he hasn't been on good terms with the Mohawk management, especially with Coach Hansen. He's been going around with a chip on his shoulder and drawing penalties in recent games, to the detriment of team morale.

In former years, Duke rarely, if ever, saw the inside of the penalty box.

It is too bad if the veteran feels he must resort to rough playing to hang on, now that he is unable to keep up with the pace.

Every one in hockey seems to realize that Duke is all washed up except Duke Blake himself.

When Duke read that, he crumpled the paper into a ball and hurled it savagely across the room.

"Washed up!" he snorted. "To read that, you'd think I was ninety-two years old and went around on crutches. I'll show them that I'm not washed up."

Duke was not being fair when he refused to recognize the truth of the article. He did not realize that he was close to the end of the hockey trail. He had been kidding himself that he still had several years of pro hockey in his legs. Hockey was the most precious thing in life to him and he was desperately hanging on. High strung and temperamental, he had indeed been carrying a chip on his shoulder.

Part of this was Hansen's fault. There were faults on both sides. Hansen had no imagination. He saw only a player who hadn't lived up to expectations and handled Duke as he would have handled any clumsy rookie.

When the Mohawks came back from their road trip, Duke Blake played a few shifts in a game against the Atlantics.

Grimly determined to show the world that he was far from through, Duke set a terrific pace from the moment he stepped out on the ice. It didn't last.

Towards the end of the second period, he was tired and spent. The Atlantics broke through his line for two goals.

In the third period, Duke could hardly crawl around the ice and the opposition rattled two more goals past the Mohawk goalie to win a 5-4 game that the Mohawks should have taken with ease.

After that, the Mohawk management let it be known they'd be willing to trade Blake. "And you can bet your bottom dollar we won't get a nibble," Hansen told Duke sourly.

"That's what you think," returned Duke confidently. "Will I be glad to get off this team of yours!"

"It's mutual!" snapped Hansen.

It was a severe shock to Duke's pride when club after club indicated a total lack of interest. He resented hockey and everyone connected with it.

"It isn't a game," he told Keeley hotly one night. "It's just a business. It takes everything you can give and then kicks you out. I'm telling you, when it comes time to talk contract with the Mohawks next year, forget everybody but yourself. They'll never thank you for being decent."

Starrett called Duke into the office the next morning. "We've made a deal for

you, Duke," he said curtly. "You're going back to the Flyers."

Duke's face brightened. This was a better break than he had ever expected. So Al Metzer was practically admitting that he had made a mistake in letting him go!

"It isn't Metzer," said Starrett, reading Duke's thoughts. "Metzer wouldn't touch you. But he's out now, and there's a new crowd running the Flyers. Joe Considine is the new manager."

"Great!" said Duke. Considine had been his old coach.

"Don't kid yourself that they're counting on much from you. I guess Considine figures you're still a drawing card so far as the fans in his town are concerned. It's a cinch you're no drawing card anywhere else. It's a straight trade. We're getting young Harrigan in exchange, and it wouldn't be a deal if I didn't think we're ahead by it."

"Away ahead," remarked Hansen, who was lounging near the window.

Duke Blake looked at the pair with a sardonic smile. "You can't make me mad," he said. "You just watch, Starrett. And you, too, Hansen. You think you're getting rid of a has-been and getting a young guy with plenty of hockey ahead of him. If there's a team in the league that I'll be anxious to lick when I get back to the Flyers, it's this outfit of yours. Maybe you won't be so smug about this trade by the time the season is over."

He shouldn't have said it, of course. The Mohawks had handled him badly and had humiliated him. But Duke was bitter about that trade. To think that he, Duke Blake, who was once worth a record price was being traded for an untried rookie, with no cash consideration. This was hard to swallow. His quick temper got away from him.

"Yeah?" said Hansen dryly. "Well, we don't think Considine is kidding himself that he's getting a hockey player. He just figures there's a few fans in his town who'll pay money at the box office to have a look at you before you're put away in moth-balls. Sort of a circus bet, like the bearded lady."

Hansen was deliberately insulting.

Duke flushed. "I'd like to see the Mohawks and the Flyers tangle in the finals this year," he said, "just so I could ram those words right down your throat."

Considine had always felt that the Flyers had acted hastily and unwisely in getting rid of Duke Blake, and he was glad to get the veteran back. He believed Duke had some good hockey left in him. But the new manager's chief desire was to appease the fans who had been angry when Duke had been dumped off the Flyer team after years of brilliant service.

Then again, he argued, Duke was still a drawing card. In his home city, Duke still had a big following.

And so Duke Blake came back to the Flyers. Thousands of fans greeted his return with a full-throated roar of welcome on the night Duke stepped out again in his old uniform. He turned in a good game, showing some of his old speed and trickery, and rammed in one brilliant goal.

"How's that for a comeback?" he chuckled to Alex after the game.

"Great, Duke."

"I'm as good as I ever was. Never did feel at home playing for any other outfit except the Flyers. Just watch me go for the rest of the season."

But as the schedule went on, Duke didn't figure very prominently in the Flyer victories. Young McMunn, the first-string center, was burning up the league in his first year in the majors.

Ranking third in the scoring race when the regular schedule ended, it was McMunn's punch on the attack that brought the Flyers out in front in the elimination games between second- and third-place sectional winners, up into the finals.

And there, waiting them as league champions, were the Mohawks.

Duke Blake had never forgotten that humiliating moment when Hansen had taken him out of the line-up in front of a Flyer crowd. He had never forgotten the humiliation of being dropped from the road trip, and the wisecracks of Hansen and Starrett when he had been traded back to his old team. And now, Duke Blake was glad.

"Here's my chance for revenge, kid," he told Alex. "Last thing I told Hansen was that I hoped I'd meet them in the finals, just so I could make him eat some of the remarks he made about me."

No player on the Flyer squad was more eager for victory than Duke when they met the Mohawks in the first game of the series. It was more than a game to him now; it was a personal grudge he had to settle.

When he skated out early in the opening period and got set for the face-off, he glanced contemptuously at the man opposite him. The rival center was Harrigan, the rookie whom the Mohawks had accepted in the trade that sent Duke back home.

Harrigan was nervous, a little awed by Duke's reputation. It was an easy matter to beat Harrigan to the draw, to snap the puck up and wheel away with it. Duke was like a high-spirited race horse as he broke away.

Harrigan was alongside, crowding him, trying to get the puck. Duke played with the youngster, suddenly pivoted and left Harrigan flat-footed. Duke then rammed a pass over to right wing and streaked in fast, grabbed the return as he moved around a defenseman, and let loose a shot backed by every ounce of power in his arms and shoulders.

(continued on page 61)

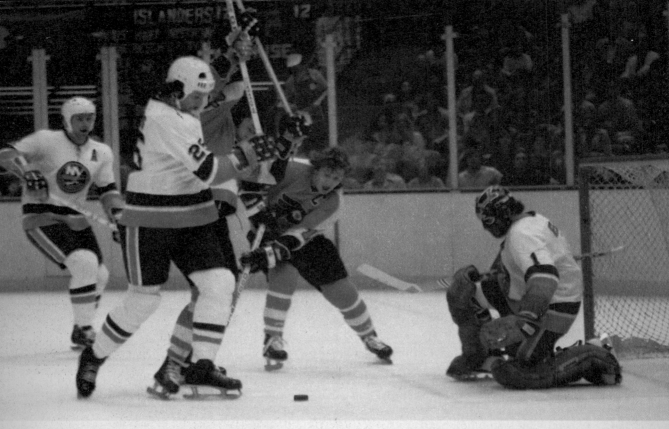

From being 3-0 down the Islanders came back to fight a thrilling seventh game against the Flyers.

The Flyers won the Stanley Cup in Buffalo on May 27.

THE FLYERS WIN AGAIN

Nowhere in hockey is victory sweeter than in Philadelphia.

After winning the Stanley Cup in 1974, the Flyers came right back to capture it again in 1975. Quaker City fans showed they did not take a second championship for granted when they poured into the streets to hail their heroes, back from Buffalo with Lord Stanley's ancient trophy, won there on the sticky evening of May 27.

A record 2.5 million Philadelphians filled the avenues to cheer the Flyers as they embarked on a five-mile motorcade which ended at John F. Kennedy Stadium. There, 100,000 fans fought for seats to hear brief words from Flyers' coach Fred Shero, owner Ed Snider, team captain Bobby Clarke and goaltending star Bernie Parent.

Fred Shero was the first person introduced and after an ovation he commented: "This is better than heaven. I'm the luckiest guy in the world. I've had three lucky days, the day I got married, the day we won last year and last night when we won again."

Clarke told the huge audience, the largest to jam the stadium since a Catholic mass in 1926: "We love you all."

Parent at first declined to speak but when the cheering did not subside he said: "Oui, Oui, we did it again. We'll see you here again next May."

The Stanley Cup, donated in 1893 as a symbol of hockey supremacy, and victim of some rather bizarre treatment over the years, was delivered in a manner that should not surprise anyone conversant with its history. It arrived wrapped in a green garbage bag and covered with a blanket.

The final series with Buffalo, played later in the season than ever before, produced some unique touches. In Buffalo, fog over the ice caused numerous delays in game three, won by Buffalo in overtime.

A low-flying bat made a brief solo flight over the ice and was hastily executed by Jim (Batman) Lorentz of the Sabres, much to the chagrin of thousands of television viewers. Later, at home, Mrs. Lorentz admonished her husband for unnecessary cruelty.

Buffalo, throughout the six games played, had trouble in goal and problems on the power play.

The tenacious checking of the Flyers, excellent balance and the customary Shero-inspired discipline guided them to victory, 4 games to 2.

Parent's shutout goaltending in the final game, and goals from Bob (Mad Dog) Kelly and Tom Clement gave the Flyers the 2-0 win they sought on foreign ice.

Their margin wasn't wide but it was adequate. Just enough to touch off another wild victory celebration in Philadelphia.

And let's not forget Kate Smith. Her mysterious influence over Flyer opponents held up again in key playoff games. In the seventh and deciding semi-final game between Philadelphia and the New York Islanders, Kate made a personal appearance at the Spectrum to sing "God Bless America." Naturally, the Flyers won and advanced against Buffalo.

The Sabres, quite conscious of the fact they had never won a game at the Spectrum (losing 13 and tying two), had the additional burden of contending with Kate's warbling in game five of the final series.

No personal appearance was needed this time. Kate's recording did the trick. The Sabres played their worst game of the playoffs and Kate's splendid statis-tics rose to 44 wins, three losses and a tie.

If Buffalo had an edge anywhere, it was in the battle of the arena sign painters. Fans in both cities are famous for their clever and unusual signs and messages.

A Buffalo fan, noting that Flyer bad-man Dave Schultz had a record on the Philadelphia hit parade, offered the fol-lowing: **"Schultz sings? Now we know two things he can't do."**

And another, jabbing a needle at the other singer in the Philadelphia camp, strung out the following in Memorial Auditorium. **"The Flyers have Kate but we've got an old bat too."**

But sign painters don't win hockey games. The Sabres' old bat, thanks to Jim Lorentz, was quickly despatched from any further playoff activity.

And a few days later, the Sabres fol-lowed suit.

Setting An example

What kind of so called "grown-ups"
Are those who choose to thrust
Such mean and angry words of hate
On little guys like us?

We skate so hard to make that goal
Like we are told to do,
But folks yell "Get him! Kill that kid!"
And often start to boo.

We're told its sport, not win or lose
But how we play the game.
If adults want to teach what's right
Why don't they do the same?

So moms and dads, I ask you please
Leave anger at the door,
And fill the rink with brotherhood
That's really what it's for!

G.M.

Hockey Coaches Clinic Power Skating Drills

BY BILL HAYWARD
Director and Chief Instructor
Cooper Hockey Coaches' Clinics

One of the major developments in hockey coaching during the past decade has been power skating. The term is misleading. A better description might be economy skating or efficient skating.

As explained by Bill Hayward, Director and Chief Instructor for the Cooper Sport Camps and Hockey Coaches' Clinics, power skating means to "get the most from the least effort."

Says Bill: "When you stroke, you stroke for power—but you cut down on the workload because there is no waste in your skating."

As taught by Bill to thousands of hockey players and coaches from professional level (Toronto Maple Leafs, Minnesota North Stars), to amateur (Toronto Marlboros, Pembroke Lumber Kings), power skating is based on a scientific system of exercises developed over the years specifically for hockey. It makes its major contributions in two main areas: self-confidence and balance.

Bill breaks the program down into three major segments:

1. A proper hockey warmup.
2. Power skating exercises which are designed to create power, agility and balance.
3. Conditioning skating, which produces both muscle and heart-wind endurance.

"Depending on whom you listen to, skating is anywhere from 75 to 95 per cent of the game of hockey," says Bill. "A weak skater isn't going to get very far in this sport.

"Power skating is designed to help the player become the most proficient skater he can in the shortest period of time.

"As used by the pros, it is both a warmup for the major and minor skating muscles, and a development process for general skating coordination, timing, balance and agility. It gets them back to top level quickly at the beginning of the season.

"For the young player, aged five to eleven years, it helps to develop their overall skating ability; it can make them better all-round skaters.

"For the developing player aged 12 to 21, it establishes a better and more powerful stride form, a more fluid skating movement, better balance and agility, and increases their confidence in their own ability to skate."

POWER SKATING is rhythm, power skating is balance, power skating is confidence and power skating is condition. It is all these things because it is a complete method of skating. Take any one of them away, and the player is incomplete as a total skater.

It is a major development in hockey because it utilizes so many of the methods of improving these factors that

35

have evolved in other sports, such as figure skating. Keeping up with the times is something that hockey has neglected for too long; on the other hand, we have forgotten many of the worthwhile areas of our past skills and training methods.

You see power skating in the National Hockey League and right on down to the peewees. I look at it this way:

Rhythm
Smooth, rhythmical (steady), coordinated movement with the least effort for maximum results.

Balance
The agility, coordination and dexterity which make up a player's general balance in skating.

Confidence
A player's absolute self-confidence that he can master a multitude of varied skating skills and drills.

Power
The strength and speed the player requires for quick-breaks and powerful strides forward, backward and laterally; his go-go ability which creates in him the attitude that he could skate all day, if need be.

Conditioning
The stamina and endurance which enable the player to skate all day, if need be, and to drive himself to physiological and psychological limits. "When the going gets tough, the tough get going."

Let's get right down to work. As in all sports events, we should start with a warmup to prepare the player for game conditions. Warmup doubles as a preparation for efficient all-out effort and protection against injury.

Our warmup is designed so that it involves all the important ligaments, muscle groups and joint areas that the player will use in the game or practice situation. He gets skating agility, too, and can go straight into action from this warmup. Most coaches will probably want their players to include some free skating after these warmup exercises, however, although this is not absolutely essential.

If lack of ice time before the game precludes doing this warmup on skates, it can be adapted to the dressing room. The players can do the exercises as they put on their gear so they are prepared for action when they hit the ice.

This warmup will take from five to eight minutes. Stronger, more advanced skaters can incorporate some of the actual power skating drills into the warmup as well; this will ensure peak preparedness for the early minutes of a game when a sharp team may reap the benefit of a quick goal. You often see players like Bobby Orr doing such power skating drills as the straight leg kick to make sure they're ready to start fast.

WARMUP EXERCISES

1. Alternate toe-touch forward
Skate erect, holding stick behind head with hands at the butt and toe and legs spread as far apart as possible. As you glide slowly forward along the ice, bend forward and force left hand down towards right toe, keeping knees straight. It should be a controlled, graceful action without any hard "twist" at the bottom. When you reach full extension, reverse procedure, forcing right hand toward left toe, still gliding forward. 10-16 repetitions (5-8 each side).

2. Alternate toe-touch backward

Skate with legs straight, feet as far apart as possible, stick held out in front with hands together. As you glide *backwards* with knees locked, bend over forward and force both hands and stick to the right skate as far as possible in a slow, controlled tempo; then repeat to left side. 10-16 reps.

3. Blade scrape

This is similar to the Crotch stretch: two hands on stick, head up, one knee bent. But this time you press down hard on the *rear* skate as you glide forward, forcing the skate forward until it reaches the heel of the front skate. Then take another gliding stride and repeat to the other side. Five reps with each leg are ample. Really press down on the rear skate as if trying to scrape a layer of ice off the rink.

4. Complete stretch

Hold stick high over head, hands wide apart, arms fully extended and skates as far apart as possible. Gliding forward, bend backwards (keeping knees straight) and stretch *up* and *back* hard. Then bend forward and down as far as possible, keeping knees locked. In this bent forward position, bounce the upper body up and down three times — you should feel it in the back thighs. 5-8 reps.

5. Crotch stretch

Holding stick at the side in one hand, bend left leg and keeping right leg as straight as possible behind you with toe out and blade flat on ice (see illustration), stretch out other hand on ice. Hold this position for five seconds, gliding forward as you do so, dragging extended right leg behind you. You should feel the stretching in the groin area. Then come up and repeat to right side with left leg back. The tempo is slow and controlled. 10 reps.

37

6. Bob stretch

This is similar to the Crotch stretch shown as exercise 5. This time, however, you hold your stick in front of you with both hands. Glide forward as before, bend left leg and extend right leg behind you with blade flat on ice so you drag it along. "Bob" up and down three times with a gentle, controlled, "springy" action. Now do the same with the other leg back. 3-5 reps each leg.

7. Shoulder roll

As in the Complete stretch (exercise 4), hold stick high overhead with arms fully extended and skates wide apart. Now force stick backwards and down past your back until it touches your buttocks. Try to keep your hands in place with elbows straight. 5 reps.

8. T-split forward

Spread skates and legs as far apart as you can with knees locked, and hold a forward glide for five seconds. Pull skates gradually together, and when toes meet toes, straighten up. Do five reps slowly, then speed up for five reps. There is no pause or hold.

9. T-split backward

From the same position as exercise 8, the T-split forward, glide backwards with the knees locked. Reach forward and down as far as you can and hold for 3-5 seconds. Then straighten up slowly, and as you do pull your skates toward each other until the heels click together. 5 reps.

10. Alternate knee drop

This is very similar to exercise 1, the Alternate toe-touch forward. However, instead of keeping the legs straight as you bend forward to touch left hand and stick to the right toe, allow the left knee to bend so that it touches the ice. The right knee will have to bend slightly as well. Hold for 3-5 seconds as you glide forward, then stand erect and repeat to other side. 5-8 reps.

11. Back dip

Glide backwards with skates wide apart, stick held behind you in the low back area just on top of the buttocks. Leaning back, push head and upper back as far backwards as possible. Knees are allowed to flex on this one. Be sure to wear a helmet in case you crash out. 5-8 reps.

POWER SKATING DRILLS

1. Straight leg kick

This is one of the great Eddie Shore exercises which helps to develop balance. It's a favorite of Bobby Orr, probably the best balanced athlete in hockey.

Stand with stick held forward at shoulder height, hands wide apart. The stick must stay in place during the exercise; it should not be tossed about. The body and head are kept erect and the player should lean back slightly when kicking.

Kick right leg up to the side at about a 45 degree angle to meet stick, keeping knee straight. The trick is to *control* the leg on the way back down — do not simply let it drop, but lower it to the ice.

When the skate touches, the left leg automatically kicks up to the left side at a 45 degree angle.

This exercise must be performed rhythmically, like a dancer doing a kicking routine to music. Do it five times each leg while gliding forward, then turn around and do it five times backwards.

2. March on ice

Hold stick in same position as in Straight leg kick, but this time when you glide forward lift knee at a 45 degree angle to the side. Hold in place as high as possible for 10-15 seconds. As soon as skate touches the ice again lift other knee. 10 reps (5 each leg). Now turn around and do it backwards.

3. High knee prance

From the March on ice, move right into this one, which is similar except that the action is speeded up: there's no hold of the high knee. You prance across the ice, driving up off the toe of skate and emphasizing the high knee lift as you prance along at a speedy tempo for 10 to 15 seconds. Reverse direction and repeat.

4. Leg balance

With both hands on stick, go down in a deep squat, thrusting right leg forward into the air and gliding forward as long as you can, pointing the toe. Then come up and try to squat on the other leg. 3 reps each leg. Try it backwards too.

This is a difficult test of balance until you get the knack. The secret is to keep the seat down in the squat — if you lean forward you will be unable to get your leg out in front of you properly.

5. Power jumps

From a deep squat position with two hands on stick in front of you, jump as high as you can. Land with legs in the same deep squat position — not with straightened legs — so you are ready for another immediate jump. 3-5 reps.

6. Back crossover

This is done in three progressions; master each one before moving on to the next. Unlike the illustration, both hands should be kept on the stick for better body control. All these are done while skating backwards with a crossover action from a half to a full length of the rink.

Progression 1: While gliding backwards on the left skate, lift right skate about six inches off the ice at a 45 degree angle to the side. Delay slightly, then bring it back across the left skate to the ice. As soon as it touches, the other skate comes up and is lifted to the side, etc.

Progression 2: Same as (1) except skate is lifted higher — 18 to 24 inches (knee over knee) — and when it is brought across the idea is to bring the right knee across the left knee before skate touches down.

Progression 3: Done as in (1) and (2) except whole leg is kicked up as high as possible, and leg crosses over the other leg on way down.

7. Walk on ice
Extend arms and stretch body as tall as possible. Keeping high on toes of skates, walk from goal line to blue line. Then change to a *running* action to the center line. Stop.

Now start to *walk* again on toes, but this time pivot completely around as you do. Spin-walk to the next blue line, then switch to a spin-run to the goal line.

Turn and repeat to other end of rink, this time spinning in the opposite direction. Remember to stretch upwards as high as possible at all times.

The players can yell during the running drill as if their team has just won the game.

8. Squat on ice
This drill comes in two parts: long squat and deep squat. The long squat is first.

Holding stick in both hands at shoulder height and gliding forward, go down in as deep a squat as possible. Then straighten up and repeat 5-10 times. Next, do it backwards.

The deep squat is done by going into a deep squat and staying there, then bouncing up and down a few inches from the knees. Bounce five times, come erect, skate a few strides to relax the muscles, then repeat. Five reps forward, three backwards.

9. Lateral crossover
This is designed to develop lateral skating strength and agility, so important in checking or taking out a player who is trying to cut past you to the side. To learn the drill, walk through it until you develop the coordination.

Stand with both hands on stick about

shoulder width apart and waist high. Walk to the left by lifting right knee and crossing it over the left knee, putting skate down about a foot outside the left skate. When it touches the ice lift left skate and place it out to the side of the right skate so you are in position to do the crossover again. Continue in this way so you move laterally across the ice. Now try it to the other side.

Keep the head up and eyes front at all times.

When you've mastered the movement, you're ready to do the exercise fast. The point to remember is that it is not simply a run to the side—the knees must be lifted high so that you do the crossover with a prancing action like a high-stepping horse. Keep head up and eyes forward.

Prance to your left the width of the rink, then to the right. 1-3 reps each way.

10. Forward crossover
Hold stick in front of you with both hands. Lift right knee high and out to the side at a 45 degree angle as you glide forward. Bring the knee high across the body and over the other knee (as you did in the Black crossover, drill 6) so that your skate touches the ice well outside the left skate. The hip should follow through over the balancing leg. As soon as the skate touches the ice the left knee comes up and crosses over the right knee. 5-10 reps with lots of control and form.

11. Leg beats
A greater developer of skating confidence, this is a variation of drill 2, the March on ice. Starting position is the same, but this time you lift left leg and skate up slowly as high as you can. Keeping the knee high and in place, kick five times slowly with the skate before returning skate to ice. Repeat with right leg. 3-5 reps each side gliding forward, then 3-5 reps backwards. It's a slow-motion action with grace and control, like a chorus line dancer.

As a variation, lift knee high, hold five seconds, then kick lower leg out straight, return to high knee bend, hold five seconds and drop leg slowly to ice. Repeat with other leg. 3-5 reps each leg.

12. Ice rip
Holding stick in front of you, do a quarter squat. Then twist the body to the left so that the heel of your right skate cuts a tight "C" in the ice in front of you. Really "rip" the ice with it. Repeat quickly with the other skate so that you move forward across the ice. Use lots of power and speed but keep skate action short so

that you make small "C's" instead of wide ones. The weight is on the heels of the skates. Continue for 10-15 secs.

Now do the same thing backwards. You'll have to lean forward and the "rip" will be done with the toe instead of the heel. It's not simply a backward skate but a twist and "rip" (C-cuts) with a short, forcing action. The weight is on the toes of the skates.

You should really feel this exercise in the quadriceps muscles of the thigh just above the knee.

13. T-balance
A figure skating exercise for balance, body control and leg stretch. Hold stick in front of you with the hands underneath. Lift left leg straight out behind, leaning body forward until the leg and body form a straight line parallel with ice. Hands and stick are extended. Try to straighten right leg so it is locked at knee. Glide forwards for 3-5 seconds, change legs and repeat 3-5 times each leg.

Note: In all these exercises remember that continuous smooth, controlled, slow movements are important. Violent, jerky action is a no-no. Get this mental picture: graceful movement as in a slow motion film.

A word to coaches and players utilizing these drills for the first time. A learning factor is involved. Players may be discouraged at first because they cannot do the drills properly. However, they will learn quickly. Where ice time is limited, these exercises can be taught off ice so that players can get right into them when they don skates.

It should be remembered that the effectiveness of such drills is not measured by the length of time they are done, but by *how well* they are done. The rhythm and coordinated grace of the exercises are important. Five minutes of correct performance are better than 15 minutes of sloppy, lackadaisical and uncontrolled effort.

It helps if the player visualizes himself doing the warmup exercises rhythmically in slow motion. There should be no sudden, awkward movements.

One of the best lines from last season's playoffs was uttered by Vancouver goalie Gary Smith. Commenting on his 5'5" teammate, Bobby Lalonde, Smith said: "He'd be great in a short series."

Pete Stemkowski: (To reporters) "Hey, guys! I want you to know I'm on a seafood diet."
Reporters: "What's that?"
Stemkowski: "A seafood diet? When I see food I want to eat it."

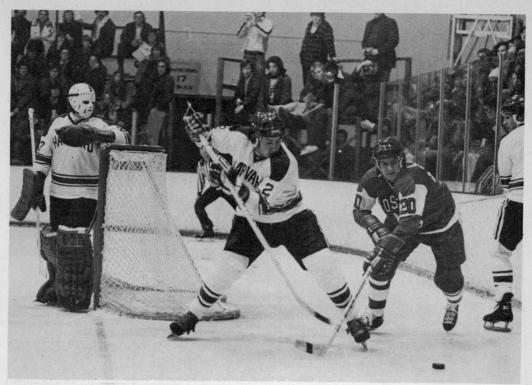

University hockey is always thrilling.

Herb Brooks, Minnesota coach, exults after a Minnesota victory.

44

Stickhandling Through Life

It's Easier When You Finish School

BY BRIAN McFARLANE

I'm one of the lucky ones. I was able to cram my life full of hockey and still get an education. Sometimes I shudder to think how easily I might have been persuaded to pass up a chance at a college education in favor of a pro hockey career, most likely in the minor leagues.

You see, I was a fair sort of junior player. One year our team played 20 playoff games leading to the Memorial Cup only to be eliminated by a Quebec team paced by Jean Beliveau. I also had a fling at the tough OHA junior league and I once attended a Chicago Black Hawks' tryout camp. I worked hard at my hockey because I loved the game. I still love it.

Oh, it would have been nice to be as good as Beliveau or some of the other top juniors of that era, fellows I played against like Leo Labine, Glen Hall, Pierre Pilote, Ken Wharram, Alex Delvecchio, Camille Henry and others.

But somehow I knew, even if I turned pro, that I would never be in a class with the great players in the game.

So it was easy for me to accept when I was offered a scholarship to St. Lawrence University in Canton, New York. I often say it was the smartest decision I ever made.

College opened all kinds of doors for me, just as it has for hundreds of other young Canadians. It was so much more enjoyable than high school. For the first

time in years nobody had to stand over me prodding me to study.

I was seldom bored and my renewed interest in education was reflected in my grades. Aside from working in the

Keith Magnuson: Chicago Black Hawk star knows the value of an education. He graduated from the University of Denver before turning pro.

45

Today all college players are scouted by the pros.

cafeteria to help pay my way, I also found time to get involved in campus politics, to become a disc jockey on the campus radio station, and to act in a college play.

As for combining education with hockey, it was no trouble at all. In college, we played about 25 games each year and worked out for a couple of hours a day during the season.

The fact we had a good team helped make it much more enjoyable. In two of the four years I played at St. Lawrence we went to the NCAA finals at Colorado Springs.

In those days, few pro scouts gave a second glance to college players. A few years later, when Bill Hay and Red Berenson proved that top college players could become top pros, the scouts showed a lot more interest. Today, with expansion, an outstanding college player will have an easy time of it catching on with a pro club. That is, if he still wants to make hockey a career.

In my case, college life introduced me to broadcasting and I decided to pursue some goals in that direction. Mind you, I didn't put hockey completely in the background when I graduated. I tried refereeing and even acted as player-coach of a semi-pro team in Schenectady, New York for a season.

Over the course of a season I talk with hundreds of young players. I tell them all the same thing. Play hockey and enjoy it. But don't put it ahead of education. Despite hockey expansion, only a select few players who turn professional make it all the way to the top. The intelligent young man today will maintain good grades in school and still find time to play hockey.

In almost every case, the student-athlete who accepts an opportunity to play hockey at the college level, in Canada or the United States, will look back in later years and say, "Those four years in college were the happiest days of my life."

46

St. Lawrence scores against Middlebury. College hockey has grown dramatically since this photo was taken in the early fifties. The author is number 12.

College brings a young man (or woman) into a vast world of knowledge, intelligence and specialized training difficult to find in any other environment.

The spectrum of the professional hockey world is not nearly so broad, offering money, travel, glamor for the most part. Admittedly, those are attractive factors. The concerned, intelligent pro hockey player often pursues his education on a part-time basis but this takes great self-discipline. In fairness, it should be noted that some individual pro clubs offer encouragement and assistance in helping a player toward a college degree. And the National Hockey League has, for the past few summers, conducted special university courses in Ottawa for the professional player eager to learn. But they are sparsely attended.

It's difficult for a player, having finished a gruelling 80-game schedule plus playoffs, to recapture proper learning habits and apply himself to concen-

trated study when his mind and body urge him to relax and enjoy the vacation so well-earned.

Some young players, contemplating a college career, question the ability of college hockey coaches. It's been my experience that the majority of them are quite good. Some are former pros, many are not. That has little to do with their ability to teach or coach at the college level.

Billy Cleary, coach at Harvard, was a brilliant player twenty years ago and starred on the 1960 U.S. Olympic team, winners at Squaw Valley. He passed up pro hockey offers and now is regarded as one of the top coaches in college ranks. He has studied the game with an intensity that most pro coaches envy.

The same might be said of Herb Brooks, coach at Minnesota, 1974 U.S. college champions and runners-up to powerful Michigan Tech last season.

Ned Harkness, coach at little RPI in Troy, New York and later coach at Cornell, was often called "the Toe Blake of

47

the college leagues" — just about the highest praise a man could get. Harkness' biggest star at Cornell was goalie Ken Dryden and Dryden still considers Harkness, despite a couple of troubled years in pro hockey at Detroit, to be an outstanding mentor of young players. Now back in college hockey, Harkness is starting from scratch at Union College in Schenectady, N.Y. With Ned at the helm, you'll be hearing from Union. Just wait.

In Canada, the college coaches get less recognition than their U.S. counterparts but they are equally as competent. And like the U.S. coaches, they are concerned about their players' progress in all aspects of life. Generally, college coaches are keenly interested in a player's development as a man, unlike many pro coaches who's sole interest often seems to be in a players ability to produce . . . on the ice.

Give college hockey a thought. And if you ever get the opportunity, ask Bobby Hull, Gordie Howe or any of the other old pros. Ask them if there's one thing they regret about the pattern of their lives. Most of them will tell you the same thing.

They wish they'd finished school.

Dave Keon is coming off the ice after practice and I ask him about the number of times the Leafs have been penalized for having too many men on the ice. Why do teams get caught like that?

"Sheer stupidity," replies the captain. "Somebody's just not thinking or paying attention in that situation. Sometimes it's the player on the bench not being ready to jump over the boards at the proper moment so another player jumps on in his place. Then the first player jumps on too and we're caught. Or it could be the player on the ice waves at the bench for relief. On his way to the bench he gets a break and takes off with the puck. Meanwhile, another player has jumped on the ice to spell him off and we're caught again. More than anything, stupidity leads to such penalties."

Is it ever the coach's fault I wanted to know, thinking back a few years when Ned Harkness coached Detroit and the Wings led the league in such penalties. Many critics blamed Harkness at the time for the remarkable number of bench penalties compiled by Detroit for having too many men on the ice.

"No, you can't blame the coach," said Keon thoughtfully. "Not in our case at least. It's the players' responsibilty to be alert and avoid such penalties."

PEE-WEE AND HIS PALS *by Bill Reid*

48

True or False?   (Answers at the back of the book)

1. When Mickey Redmond scored 52 goals in the 1972-73 season he became the first Detroit player to accomplish that feat.

    True ( )   False ( )

2. Philadelphia Flyers were the first winners of the Clarence S. Campbell Bowl which went to the first place finishers in the West Division in 1967-68.

    True ( )   False ( )

3. Dave Keon's first NHL team was the New York Rangers.

    True ( )   False ( )

4. Punch Imlach once started in the NHL as a forward with Detroit.

    True ( )   False ( )

5. When Gordie Howe retired as an active player his famed number 9 was retired by the Detroit organization.

    True ( )   False ( )

6. Boston's Phil Esposito began his career in the NHL as a member of the Chicago Black Hawks.

    True ( )   False ( )

7. Billy Reay, Chicago coach, was once a player for the Montreal Canadiens.

    True ( )   False ( )

8. The line of Ken Hodge, Phil Esposito and Wayne Cashman accounted for a record 140 goals in 1970-71.

    True ( )   False ( )

9. Bryan Watson of the Pittsburgh Penguins was the NHL "Bad Man" of the 1971-72 season.

    True ( )   False ( )

10. Stan Mikita of Chicago won the NHL scoring championship on four occasions.

    True ( )   False ( )

The Ultimate Outdoor Rink

Hockey is booming in the United States. Thousands of young players are enjoying the game, playing wherever they can find ice. And ice time is often difficult to find.

That's why Dr. Robert Pike, a physician and surgeon in Delmar, New York, decided he'd emulate an old Canadian custom — and build a backyard rink for his sons and the kids in the neighborhood.

It started about six years ago. Dr. Pike, an ardent skier, outfitted his three youngsters with ski equipment. He even developed a small ski run in his backyard. One day there was a particularly heavy rainfall which froze quickly, forming a small patch of ice at the bottom of the slope. Dr. Pike cleaned the snow off the ice and the kids spent one entire day skating.

"That weekend," says Dr. Pike, "I

Time to pick sides and have a game.

Jeff Pike plays goal.

Mrs Susan Kimberley.

Mrs Kimberley gives a figure skating lesson to her daughter, Mary, and Dr Pike's daughter, Susan.

52

asked the kids if they wanted to go skiing with me as they usually did. To my surprise they said no. They preferred to stay home and skate in the backyard. That was all right with me so I got out the garden hose and flooded the area, enlarging it. Then my brother-in-law, who was quite a good high school hockey player, dug out a couple of hockey sticks and began showing some of the boys the fundamentals of hockey.

"That was the beginning. Since then, the rink just kept getting bigger and bigger and now it's pretty much the hub of our recreational activity in wintertime."

The following summer, Dr. Pike and a friend borrowed a bulldozer and graded a portion of the yard, doubling the area for flooding in the winter. A concrete block rim was added to contain the water and to act as a rebound when the boys played hockey. All the kids in the area help with upkeep and maintenance. At the end of each hockey session, the boys scrape the snow off the ice so that Dr. Pike can flood the surface in the chill of the evening. No scrape . . . no flood. That's the rule and it's strictly adhered to.

One half of the Pike garage has been converted into a hockey dressing room, with benches and storage space for skates and equipment. If there's any spare equipment around, any child is welcome to use it as long as it fits.

The kids are justifiably proud of the new goal posts they built last year. One Sunday, when it was too warm to skate, they laid out some patterns and spent the afternoon bending pipes and making goal frames. One of the boys asked his shop teacher if the goals could be welded, primed and painted as a school project. With the full cooperation of the school, it was done.

Finding nets to fit the goals was no problem. When asked to contribute to this cause, local parents chipped in with

The new goals. This was a neighborhood project.

generous amounts, more than enough to purchase the best professional nylon nets available. With the surplus, Dr. Pike purchased other equipment, such as pucks, shovels and similar necessities.

The hockey program in the Pike backyard has produced some interesting results. John Pike, 14, is a first-line forward at Albany Academy and Jeff, 10 plays for the Squirt All Stars in Troy, New York.

There's something for the girls, too. Susan Kimberley, an excellent figure skater residing in the area, volunteered to give lessons. Susan's informal classes keep growing all the time.

And so, it seems, does that backyard rink. Dr. Pike won't admit it, but chances are he's pondering ways to install higher boards, a complete lighting system and who knows, perhaps he's even checked out the cost of a Zamboni.

He doesn't get to ski much anymore, but any regrets he may have are quickly dissipated when a pink-cheeked youngster skates up to him, skids to a stop, and says, "Gee, Dr. Pike. That's a super hockey rink you made for us to play on."

HOUSTON

Repeats in Avco Cup Series

The Houston Aeros, paced by the brilliant goaltending of rookie Ron Grahame, and the offensive thrusts of Gordie Howe, the ageless wizard, swept to their second consecutive Avco Cup championship by whipping the Quebec Nordiques in four straight games last May.

Houston won the WHA final series with ease and a Quebec City crowd of 8,426 gave Howe and his mates a standing ovation when the final buzzer ended game four.

It was a fine tribute to Howe, one of the world's most amazing athletes, who will soon be 48 years old, and who earlier stated he will call it quits after the Aeros opening game in 1975-76.

Howe scored eight goals in the playoffs, two less than his son Mark.

Ron Grahame, the rookie netminding sensation from the University of Denver, collected 10 straight playoff wins and was voted the Most Valuable Player in the post-season matchups.

After WHA president Dennis Murphy presented the Avco Cup to Houston team captain Ted Taylor, Gordie Howe awarded the Gordie Howe trophy to Grahame. The Howe award, a new one, goes to the playoff MVP.

"The kid made it easy for all of us," said Howe. "He's a great goalie and like all of the great ones he seems to play his best when the pressure is on."

Grahame turned in his strongest effort in the entire series with Quebec in the second period of the final game. He faced 18 shots and was beaten only once by Rejean Houle.

Like the Philadelphia Flyers, the Aeros won their title away from home. Unlike Philadelphia, there was no mammoth celebration in Houston when the victors returned home. Several hundred fans turned out at the airport to greet the Aeros. And wouldn't you know...team captain Ted Taylor dropped the shiny trophy as he was coming off the plane, damaging it slightly.

'Heck, that's nothing to worry about," said Taylor. "We'll get it fixed up pretty soon. After all, we've got it for at least another year."

PEE-WEE AND HIS **PALS** *by Bill Reid*

54

LAST SEASONS ROOKIES

Will They Shine As Sophomores?

"As far as the Calder Trophy is concerned, some guys will tell you they don't really care if they win it or not. Well, I care. It's a great honor to win this award. I wouldn't be honest if I didn't say I want to win it."

—ERIC VAIL, ATLANTA FLAMES

Suddenly their names were household words. At least they were in hockey households. Pierre Larouche, Eric Vail, Bob Hess, Clark Gillies, Doug Risebrough, Rick Middleton, Ron Greschner, Dave Hrechkosy, Danny Gare.

They were last season's rookies ... class of 1974-75.

Larouche, the slick Pittsburgh centerman, collected more points than any other freshman, 68, to beat out Buffalo's Danny Gare, who finished with 62 and Atlanta's Eric Vail, who wound up with 60.

Vail topped the goal scorers with 39 despite missing eight games with a damaged wrist. Gare played in 78 games and collected 31 goals but missed a lot of ice time whenever the Buffalo Sabres employed their power play or killed penalties.

Middleton broke a bone in his leg and played in only 47 games. Still, he scored 22 goals and might have topped 40 barring injury.

Greschner, a strong young Ranger defenseman, finished well up in the rookie scoring race and Larry Sacharuk of St. Louis, another rookie rearguard, scored an impressive 20 goals. His teammate, Bob Hess, impressed everyone with his poise and ability to lug the puck up the ice from his defense position.

Dave Hrechkosy of the Seals finished with 29 goals while Clark Gillies of the Islanders (25 goals) and Doug Risebrough of the Canadiens tied for points with 46.

It was a fine rookie crop and here's the way they finished in the points race.

Top 15 Rookie Scorers 1974-75

	GP	G	A	Pts
Pierre Larouche, Pittsburgh .	79	31	37	68
Danny Gare, Buffalo	78	31	31	62
Eric Vail, Atlanta	72	39	31	60
Clark Gillies, Islanders	80	25	22	47
Doug Risebrough, Montréal ..	64	15	32	47
Larry Patey, California	79	25	20	45
Ron Greschner, Rangers	70	8	37	45
Dave Hrechkosy, California .	72	29	14	43
Peter McNab, Buffalo	53	22	21	43
Al MacAdam, California	80	18	25	43
Larry Sacharuk, St. Louis	76	20	22	42
Rick Middleton, Rangers	47	22	18	40
Mario Tremblay, Montréal ..	63	21	18	39
Bob Bourne, Islanders	77	16	23	39
Bob Hess, St. Louis	76	9	30	39

The post-season balloting for rookie-of-the-year and the coveted Calder Trophy was a close one. Members of the Hockey Writers' Association finally settled on Eric Vail of the Atlanta Flames.

Second in the voting was Pierre Larouche of Pittsburgh Penguins and third place was captured by Danny Gare.

With their rookie season behind them, the question is: How many of these players are shining as sophomores? How many of them will hone their game to the point where they become bona fide hockey superstars?

As for the rookies who struggled through their freshmen year, they would do well to draw encouragement from hockey's history book. It reveals that many of hockey's brightest stars had similar difficulties coping with major league play. Gordie Howe, for example, scored a mere 7 goals in his rookie season with Detroit. Howie Meeker captured the Calder that year.

Rocket Richard suffered a leg injury in his rookie season and saw action in only 16 games, scoring 5 goals. Gaye Stewart won rookie honors that season. In the seasons to follow, Stewart and Meeker watched Howe and Richard zoom to super stardom.

Jean Beliveau lost out in the Calder race to little Camille Henry. Bobby Hull did not win the Calder. Neither did Richard Martin or Phil Esposito.

While this year's sophomores can look forward to future success, they might also glance back from time to time. They might discover that some of the plodders, the non-achievers in the rookie class of 1974-75, have suddenly reached hockey maturity after a year of struggle.

Let's examine some of the top rookies from last season. The following men should be hockey stars for the next fifteen years.

PIERRE LAROUCHE:

Pierre began the 1974-75 season as an 18-year old. He was the Penguins' number 1 draft choice and he played his junior hockey in Sorel, Quebec. During his final season in Sorel, Pierre established an all-time junior scoring mark of 94 goals and 157 assists for 251 points. The old record of 130-79-209 was set by Guy Lafleur.

The Sorel team collected an unbelievable 620 goals in a 70-game season, averaging about nine a game.

Pierre made an impressive debut in the NHL, scoring a goal against Minnesota in his first big league game. He also scored a goal in his first playoff game against St. Louis. In between, he set the pace for all NHL rookie point collectors, finishing with 68 points.

Sometimes cocky, always exuberant, Pierre credits teammate Jean Pronovost with helping him adjust to an NHL lifestyle.

"Jean says 'do this' and I do this," laughs Pierre. "When he says 'do that' I do that. How can I go wrong with a fine fellow like Jean to look after me?"

"And you know what nickname they picked out for me? Peter Puck. I just hope I can score like that Peter Puck."

Someday Pierre would like to be as valuable to the Penguins as Stan Mikita is to the Chicago Black Hawks.

That day is almost here.

ERIC VAIL:

When Eric Vail was a junior hockey star in Sudbury, Ontario, he had a coach who stuttered in tense situations. When Vail would pick up the puck in his own zone and begin barreling toward the opposition net, his coach would hang over the boards and scream:

"G,g,g, go, you, B,B,B, Big Train, go!"

The Big Train never stopped going. He was derailed for a time during his first pro season when he ran into teammate Pat Quinn and fractured a vertebrae in his back. As a result, he played in only 23 games for Atlanta, two less than the maximum allowed for rookie status.

These 23 games helped him adjust to

Eric Vail, Rookie of the Year.

NHL play, however, and in his first full season as a Flame he accomplished the following:

1. He broke Atlanta's season goal-scoring record by 12, scoring 39 goals in 72 games.

2. He scored those 39 despite missing eight games and nearly a month of the season with a broken left wrist. He still scored two of those 39 with a cast on that wrist.

3. He scored eight more goals than any other rookie in the National Hockey League, despite playing less.

4. He made his place in the NHL record books right behind Buffalo's Rick Martin as the second leading rookie goal-scorer in league history. It now reads Martin with 44 in 1971-72, Vail with 39 in 1974-75, Gil Perrault with 38 in 1970-71.

5. He scored three hat tricks (against Detroit, Kansas City and Vancouver) and had seven two-goal games.

He did not win the overall rookie scoring title. But two years ago, Atlanta's Tom Lysiak won that and finished second in the rookie balloting. Vail did not play for a playoff team. Last year, Lysiak did and Denis Potvin's Islanders finished last. Potvin still won the honors.

"Midway through last season—heck, as late as February — I was just shooting for 30 goals," says Vail, a 6'2", 210-pound left-winger out of Timmins, Ont. "I never figured I'd have any chance at the rookie award.

"All I know is that I figure I had a pretty good year for a rookie."

So do the Flames.

DANNY GARE:
Danny Gare is a fresh-faced right winger for the Buffalo Sabres who appears young enough to belong to his own fan club. The youthful members of that club, "Gare's Gang", have much to talk about in the play of their hero from Nelson, B.C., who not only scored a goal just 18 seconds into his first big league hockey game, three seconds shy of a record, but who also played a major role in the Sabres' ascendancy to the top of the league.

Gare was near the top of the rookie scoring race all last year, but it's his all-round contribution to the Sabres that has made Buffalo General Manager Punch Imlach his staunchest supporter.

"Danny has certainly already proved he's got the makings of a top goal scorer, and his offensive play is outstanding for a rookie. But it's his checking ability which makes him an exeptional young hockey player," said Imlach.

"He was on a line (with Don Luce and Craig Ramsay) which was consistently assigned to check the opposition's top scorers, and all you have to do is look at his plus-minus figures to see what kind of a job Danny and his linemate were doing. The three of them led the club in this category.

"Danny's offense suffered sometimes, because Luce and Ramsay are the Buffalo principal penalty-killers and they were on the ice often in that role, which means Gare missed many shifts a game.

57

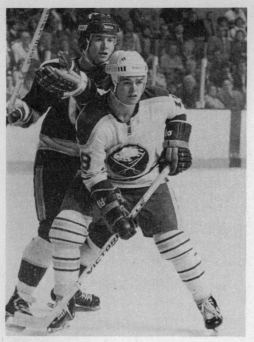

Danny Gare

You can't score when you're not on the ice.''

Gare's size and youthful appearance belie his strength on the ice. A compact skater, with one of the best wrist shots to come into the league in recent years, he's the son of the head of the physical education department at Notre Dame College in Nelson, and Danny's burly chest and shoulders show the strength exercises he's been working on for years.

Gare was drafted in the second round of the 1974 amateur-draft after a sensational junior career with the Calgary Centennials of the Western Canada Junior Hockey League. In his last junior season, Gare scored 68 goals and 59 assists, while adding 238 penalty minutes en route, and was termed "one of the finest team leaders I've ever coached" by his coach, Scotty Munro.

Gare is only 5′9″ and 175 pounds but has never let his stature cause him to back off in the corners. "Far from it," said Sabres Coach Floyd Smith. "He just puts his nose in and comes out with the puck. I not only like his aggressiveness, but the finesse part of his forechecking.''

Smith praised Gare for not becoming too aggressive in his rookie season, as well.

"Danny is scrappy and doesn't back down from anyone," Smith said, "but he does not run around taking unnecessary penalties. This means he isn't going to hurt himself or the club by spending too much time in the penalty box.''

In his first shift on the ice in a pre-season game against Philadelphia at the Spectrum, Gare was run into the boards from behind by Dave Schultz directly in front of the Flyers' bench. Gare's gloves were off and fists flying immediately and the Hammer hasn't bothered him since.

RICK MIDDLETON:
"Is that kid for real?" someone asked Marshall Johnston, then coach of the California Seals. The question followed a four-goal outburst by rookie Rick Middleton of the Rangers early last season.

"He's for real, all right," answered Johnston. "A natural goal scorer is what he is and they don't come along too often. Four goals on four shots out there tonight. That's incredible.''

Middleton was drafted (No. 1) in the 1973 amateur draft after a 67-goal season with the Oshawa juniors. He didn't catch on with the Rangers in his first season as a pro but he set the American Hockey League on fire in Providence with 36 goals and 84 points, was rookie of the year and was named to the league's first all-star team.

"There's no possible way he can miss becoming a big star in the NHL," said John Muckler, Providence coach. "He's got better moves than most of the guys I've seen in the NHL.''

Middleton admits he was extremely nervous before his first big league start.

"I thought sure I was going to throw up before the game," he recalls.

Derek Sanderson, listening, laughed. "Yeah," said Turk. "He was nervous, all right. All he did that night was score a pair of goals and turn the game in our direction. He's got it all, that kid. Tremendous moves."

By mid-January, Middleton had 22 goals and appeared headed for a 40-plus goal season. But a broken leg put him on the shelf for the rest of the season and ended his hopes of winning the Calder.

But remember the name, Middleton. He's dynamite.

RON GRESCHNER:
In his final season of junior hockey, with New Westminister Bruins of the Western Canada Hockey League, Ron Greschner teamed up with Bob Hess along the New Westminister blueline.

"Both of us would laugh out loud," he recalls, "if someone had told us we'd both be regulars in the NHL before we turned 20."

Greschner was famous in junior play for his dazzling rink-length rushes. He impressed pro scouts with 33 goals and 70 assists for 103 points, a WCHL record for defensemen. Still, Hess was regarded as the better pro prospect and went higher in the junior draft (to St. Louis).

The Rangers took 18-year old Dave Maloney, another defenseman, as their first-round choice and they hardly needed another rearguard. But Greschner was too good to pass up, and when he was still available in the second round, New York grabbed him.

Greschner is versatile. He can play the point on the New York power play or play either defense position when the Rangers are one or even two men short. Not many rookies can do that.

BOB HESS:
Late last season, St. Louis Blues coach Garry Young was asked to comment on his rookie defenseman, Bob Hess.

"Well, you can't compare anyone

with Bobby Orr," began Young, "but when you see what this kid Hess does out there you have to feel he'll be somewhere in Orr's class by the time he's 25."

Hess, at 19, has been brilliant for the Blues. In 1974-75 he established a handful of team records, including most points and most assists for a Blues' rookie. He also topped the record for most points by a defenseman, set seven years ago by Jim Roberts. Hess, the Blues' number 1 amateur draft choice in 1974, adjusted quickly to the fast pace of the NHL.

"We beat both Montreal and Boston early in the season and I felt I played well in both of those games," he recalls. "That sort of thing can give a young player great confidence."

"He's great with the puck," crows Young. "A great skater. He faces all the good moves. He meets players like Esposito, Clarke, Lafleur, Dionne, night after night and always comes out looking well."

"I was surprised to be drafted number 1 by the Blues," says Hess. "Plenty of guys in our league got more publicity than I did. But I'm sure happy to be in the NHL. It's everything I thought it would be ... the best hockey in the world."

DOUG RISEBROUGH:
It's not often that a rookie player fresh out of junior hockey breaks in with Montreal on a first-string basis. But Doug Risebrough, drafted out of Kitchener juniors in 1974, did it, thanks largely to an injury to veteran centerman Henri Richard.

Just 16 games into the 1974-75 season, with Richard out with a broken ankle, the Canadiens called up Risebrough from their Nova Scotia farm club and his buzzsaw approach to the game immediately captivated discerning Montreal fans.

"The kid is a natural leader," says veteran Don Awrey. "He reminds me a little of Bobby Clarke of Philadelphia the way he works his butt off out there. He's a talker, too. He'll tell an opponent where to get off and he'll tell a teammate to get the lead out if he thinks it'll do any good."

Risebrough explains himself. "You've got to stand up and be counted in this league. If you don't they'll knock you right on your fanny. If a rookie gets pushed and he doesn't push back the word soon gets around and he's given a label. I'm not trying to be a leader but if I have something to offer in that area so much the better. I just want to stick with this team, that's all."

There's no question Risebrough will stick.

There were many other outstanding rookies to win regular big league assignments in 1974-75.

Clark Gillies of the Islanders, by season's end, was attracting rave notices for his play. The Seals claimed two premier first-year men, Dave Hrechkosy with 29 goals and Larry Patey with 25.

Larry Sacharuk of St. Louis blasted in 20 goals and Peter McNab, despite an awkward skating stride, collected 22 goals in only 53 games.

Garry Inness played superbly in goal for Pittsburgh. Gordon McRae did likewise for Toronto late in the season and Tiger Williams provided the Leafs with some much-needed muscle.

Peter LoPresti was a bright spot for Minnesota.

Larry Goodenough of Philadelphia, Rick Hampton of the Seals, Hank Nowak of Boston, Grant Mulvey of Chicago, Wilf Paiement of Kansas City, Mario Tremblay of Montreal, Glenn Resch of the Islanders, Mike Marson of Washington and little Doug Palazzari of St. Louis: they all have talent. Many will rise to stardom. A few will even become superstars.

When King Clancy was a referee in the NHL he made a questionable call one night in Boston. Art Ross, owner of the Bruins, blasted Clancy. "What's wrong with your eyes, King?" yelled Ross.

"Nothin' at all," roared Clancy. "What's more, my eyes are insured for $75,000."

"Oh yeah," snarled Ross. "Then what did you do with the money?"

One of the fine young Soviet hockey players is a forward named Vacheslav Anisin. When a broadcaster was asked the names of Anisin's linemates, he replied with a straight face, "Excedrin and Bufferin."

One of the Buffalo Sabres likes to tell this story about Jerry Korab, the burly defenseman.

"When Jerry joined our club," says the informer, "he was given a complete medical including an eye test. And when the eye doctor asked Jerry to read the bottom line, Korab said, 'Read it! That guy's my cousin!'"

Gordie Howe has been asked some wild questions about hockey over the years. but the topper came in Houston this past winter.

Says Gordie: "One guy came up to me and asked with a straight face, how much air there was in the average hockey puck."

(continued from page 31)

There was a roar as the goalie picked it off just as it seemed bound for the upper corner. Duke went boring in when the puck was thrown to a corner. He slammed up against a Mohawk forward along the boards, fighting furiously for possession, got the puck and slapped a pass to a waiting teammate in front of the net. The goalie knocked it down and cleared far out to a Mohawk at the blue line.

Duke Blake came storming through the players in pursuit, caught his man at center, took the puck away, lost it to Harrigan, hooked it savagely away from the youngster and whirled back on the attack.

He stormed in again with the old choppy, zigzag stride and blazed another shot that just ticked the crossbar and glanced to the glass.

This game was on Mohawk home ice, and the crowd was in a howling panic lest one of those drives should count.

The fans were roaring at the Mohawks to clear, to break up the attack. But Duke was boring in again. He swooped in, his stick outstretched and just missed a pass. He turned sharply and went back. He chased Harrigan all the way down the ice, nailed the loose puck when Harrigan got into trouble at the Flyer defense, and came tearing back with it.

Duke started down on another rush. This time, a defenseman caught him off-stride, stepped into him and smeared him. He was up, a little slower now, but up in time to intercept a pass and unleash another blistering shot.

The goalie took it on the chest and came out sprawling trying to smother the rebound. Duke hurdled enemy sticks and plunged in, hacking desperately in an effort to get at the puck. Mohawk players piled themselves in a heap, and the whistle blew.

Considine, the Flyer manager, watched the feverish attack gravely. He glanced at the coach and shook his head.

"He'll burn himself out," muttered Considine. "Maybe Duke could have kept up that pace five years ago, but not now. He'll be limp as a dish rag before the game is over. Tell him to take it easy and wait for his breaks.

"He's making his own breaks," returned Kendall, the coach. "He's mighty set on beating that team, chief."

"So am I."

At the end of the shift, with the score board still blank, the lines were changed.

"Good work, Duke," said Kendall. "You're going great to-night."

Duke was panting a little. He had been going at top speed from the moment he hit the ice.

"Should have had a goal out of it."

"You'll get one yet. Take it easy. Save something for the last period."

But when Duke went out again he made no attempt to conserve his energies. He flew at the Mohawks with every ounce of speed he could muster. He made young Harrigan look foolish with his relentless checking and piledriving rushes.

Even if his timing was a little off—just off enough that the Mohawk goalie was able to play his shots safely—Duke was the spearhead of a vicious attack that drove the Mohawks in behind their own blue line and gave the crowd more anxious minutes.

When he came to the bench again his knees were trembling, but he refused to admit even to himself that the pace was telling on him. Just let him get a goal, that was all. Just let him whip one in there to score against the Mohawks and he would play a checking game for the rest of the evening.

McMunn scored for the Flyers early in the second period, scored on a beautiful end-to-end rush that earned a roar of appreciation from even a hostile crowd. And as Duke watched McMunn's swift, flashing flight down the ice towards the net and the tricky feint and backhand shot that sent the puck whizzing into the net, he felt a pang of envy.

That should have been his rush, his goal, his applause.

He had meant to save himself in the second period, but that goal of McMunn's made him forget his resolution. He tore into the Mohawks at a frantic pace when he was on the ice, skated himself ragged, came within an inch of scoring during a pile-up in front of the Mohawk net.

But he didn't quite make it, and when the line was relieved, Duke had no spring in his step as he slumped on the bench. His shoulders sagged and his nerves were quivering with weariness.

McMunn was turning in a fine game. He was not leading such wild and sustained attacks as Duke; but whenever the Flyers were in there, McMunn was always dangerous, sniping with deadly accuracy, making plays and laying down passes that spelled trouble for the enemy goalie. He had an assist on the Flyers' second goal midway through the period.

The Mohawks came back fast, hitting hard and snagged a well-earned goal close to the end of the period.

When Duke came out for his next turn in that period, he decided to wait for the breaks. He played a careful checking game, covering young Harrigan closely, saving himself, letting his wings do the rushing, hovering outside for a pass and stray pucks. But at that, his skates felt as heavy as lead when he clumped into the dressing room

"I'm not saying to play a defensive game in this period," said Kendall, before the team went back to the ice,"but take no chances. Hang onto that one-goal lead whatever you do. Watch your checks. Hang right with them. If you see an opening, if the Mohawks draw a penalty or anything like that, go right after the extra goal and put the game on ice. But protect your lead."

The Mohawks had to carry the fight to their opponents. Trailing by one goal, they stormed in on the attack right from the beginning of the period. But the Flyer forwards blocked, checked, broke up plays, and stuck to the attackers tenaciously. The defense held firm.

Duke Blake had his hands full when he faced Harrigan in this period. Harrigan was just as fast as he had been at the start of the game, and he was boring in constantly.

At the face-off, he beat Duke to the draw, stepped away from him and broke fast for the Flyer defense. Duke gave chase, but Harrigan was hard to catch.

Duke realized that he had no speed left. He was tired. The pace he had set at the beginning of the game was telling on him now. He pursued Harrigan doggedly — checking, checking, checking. That was his job now — to hold Harrigan. But the younger man was getting away from him.

Duke was beginning to flounder. Harrigan came swinging down the ice with the puck. Duke met him, tried a poke check, but Harrigan snapped a pass to the wing and flashed past him.

Duke followed Harrigan in, as the wing was ridden off to the corner. Harrigan was dodging back and forth in front of the net, waiting for a pass. Duke covered him, crowded him, but Harrigan was as slippery as an eel.

The puck came skimming out. A defenseman stabbed at it and missed. Harrigan twisted, broke clear of Duke and got his stick on the puck. A flip of the wrists and the puck zipped hard and true for the upper corner. The goalie lunged, missed, and the red light flashed.

Bedlam! The Mohawks had tied the score.

Lines were changed. No one said anything to the Duke when he slumped wearily to the bench. He had failed to hold Harrigan.

McMunn and his wings went out after the extra goal again. The pace was terrific. An attack, counter-attack, attack again. Each team kept sending new lines over the boards at nearly every face-off. The tie remained unbroken.

Duke was sent out again. He felt a little fresher after the rest, but it did not last long. Harrigan seemed to be made of iron. He ran Duke ragged. The Mohawks turned on an attack that brought them right to the doorstep and kept them there. Duke Blake was spent, done for. He couldn't hold Harrigan. Whenever he got his stick on the puck he drilled it far up the ice — anything to break the pressure of that vicious attack.

The Mohawks swarmed in again. Duke and Harrigan clashed against the boards. They fenced for the puck; Harrigan wrenched his stick free and nailed it. Duke's stick lashed out. Harrigan hooked the puck clear and lunged away. Duke plunged after him, but Harrigan left him flat-footed and blazed a shot at the goal. It bounced off the goalie's chest and bounded out just as a Mohawk swooped in on it.

The Flyer goalie came out of his net, stick swinging, but he was an instant too late. The wingman snared it, stepped around and batted the puck into an empty cage.

Now it was the Mohawk's turn to lie back and protect their lead. With five minutes to go, the Flyers had to take desperate chances. They sent out four forwards, then five, on a sustained ganging foray. But it didn't click. The Mohawks checked closely, blanketed every man.

Two minutes from the siren, with every Flyer in behind the Mohawk blue line on the attack, two Mohawk forwards broke away and streaked down the ice with no one to beat except the goalie. A fake shot, a short pass, and the puck was banged in for an extra goal.

The Mohawks skated off the ice with the first game salted safely away and confidently predicting that they would take the series in three straight.

In the Flyer dressing room, Considine encouraged his crestfallen men.

"We just didn't get the breaks tonight boys. We'll even it up in the next game."

Over in a corner someone muttered: "We'll never take them if we can't stop that guy Harrigan."

Just as Considine predicted, the Flyers won the second game and tied up the series, coming back for their two home games on even terms with their rivals.

That second game was a classic, full of everything that goes to make a good hockey battle, with the Flyers getting a shutout by the one goal.

McMunn was the hero of that game. It was his goal in the third period that gave the Flyers their victory, and he was generally admitted to be the best man on the ice. It was McMunn's first season in the big time. One of the papers said:

> McMunn is filling Duke Blake's shoes at center. While he isn't the dazzling Duke at his best, McMunn is coming along fast and may yet rank among the great players of the game.

Duke read that and it hurt. He had learned to stick strictly to the chore of holding Harrigan in check, so that he had come through the second game with credit to himself. But he was jealous when he read about McMunn filling his shoes.

"Anybody would think I am dead or out of hockey altogether," he growled, "instead of being right on the same team with him."

Duke got a great hand from the crowd when he skated out in that third game to face Harrigan. The applause gave him a pleasant glow. He had been listening to that applause for so long that it had become part of his life, like food and drink.

He did not burn himself out as he had done in the opening game, but he pressed hard, watched constantly for openings that would give him a chance to go in on goal. But young Harrigan, besides being a permanent threat on the attack, was a consistent back-checker. Duke found it hard to shake himself free of the rival center.

The Flyers scored in the opening period when McMunn worked his way through to blaze a terrific shot at the Mohawk goalie, and his right-winger swooped in to bat the rebound across the line. They grabbed another one early in the second and a Flyer wing golfed the puck through during a wild mix-up in front of the Mohawk net.

With a two-goal lead, Duke decided he could afford to let up a little on the monotonous task of covering Harrigan. He stopped the other center when Harrigan was leading a rush at mid-ice, snared the puck, and instead of passing to an open wing, broke away with it.

Harrigan overhauled him at the blue line and crowded Duke, chopping at his stick. Duke lost control of the puck and a defenseman batted it out of danger.

A little later, Duke got possession again. And again he swept down the ice. This time, he worked his way past the defense, but just as he was about to shoot, Harrigan darted in from nowhere and handed him a body check that knocked him off balance, costing him the scoring chance.

Duke was getting peeved. Harrigan's pesky checking was getting under his skin. He tried time and again to get away from the sturdy, blond youngster, but Harrigan beat him every time.

Toward the end of the period, Duke got a break. The Mohawks were buzzing around the Flyer goal like hornets.

Duke, covering Harrigan in front of the net in case of a pass, snapped up the puck as it skimmed out from the corner. He wheeled and broke fast. Harrigan was jammed up in a pushing match with the Flyers wings. Duke was in the clear. A clean sheet of ice ahead and only a defenseman and goalie to beat.

He turned on every ounce of speed he had. The roar of the crowd thundered in his ears. Center ice, blue line, the solitary defenseman waiting, crouching!

A swish of skates, and a dark figure shouldered him. A stick smacked against his own. Duke juggled the puck, pivoted, but Harrigan was right on top of him battling for possession.

Duke broke to one side. Harrigan was right with him, like a hawk after a swallow. Duke pulled every trick in the book, but he couldn't escape his tormentor. They were getting close to the boards now.

A blind rage seized him. Duke swerved suddenly and bodied Harrigan solidly and squarely, smashed him against the boards with a terrific crash.

Harrigan went down in a limp heap. The shaft of Duke's stick had scraped across Harrigan's face as he crashed and his nose was bleeding. The whistle blew shrilly.

Sullen, Duke turned away. The referee jerked a curt thumb toward the penalty box. A storm of booing rose from the Mohawk supporters, and even from some of the Flyer fans as Duke skated over to the penalty box.

"Can't take it, huh?" yelled someone.

If a goal looks like a million dollars in a championship game, a penalty is just as important. The teams are so evenly matched that the odd-man advantage is of tremendous importance. Kendall hastily sent out his penalty killers while Hansen countered with his power play unit and the Mohawks tore in on a wild goal hunt.

The Flyers held stubbornly. Their goalie made stop after stop in a rain of rubber, but with the crowd in a frenzy after a dozen close calls, the Mohawks finally belted one in.

Worse, they followed it up minutes later with another onslaught that disorganized the Flyers completely and rammed home another goal from a scramble to tie the score.

That changed the whole complexion of the game. The Flyers had to open up now, but the Mohawks were clicking beautifully and had them on the run.

A few minutes before the end of the period, the Mohawks swept down on a rush that brought three of them inside the defense, pulled the goalie out of the net and rapped in another to give them the lead.

It was a disastrous second period, and no one knew better than Duke Blake that his penalty had started the whole thing. He was aware of the veiled glances of resentment as the players rested in the dressing room.

"I think they've shot their bolt," said Kendall to his men, quietly. "You can make up that goal and go on in and win. I'd like to finish this series on home ice, remember."

"My fault coach," muttered Duke with an effort. "I let that guy Harrigan make a sucker of me."

"Forget it," said Kendall.

They went into the third period. It was fiercely battled right from the face-off. With the Mohawks hanging desperately to their slim lead, the Flyers lived up to their names as they launched a constant series of brilliant attacks.

Midway in the period, Allen, the Flyer right-winger, skated away from his check and picked up a long pass from McMunn. He went down the boards fast, swerved in toward the defense. McMunn was covered by his own check. Allen tore in, side-stepped and let drive just as the defenseman hit him.

Allen went spinning and hit the ice with a crash, but he had managed to get his shot away. The goalie grabbed at it, got his glove on the whistling disk, but couldn't hold it. The puck zipped off his fingers, hit the upright, and glanced into the back of the net.

The score was tied again, and the crowd was in a mad uproar. But Allen was still lying on the ice. He struggled to rise, got to one knee, then slumped over again. His right leg was limp.

Allen was out of the series with a fractured leg!

Kendall had to do some quick thinking, shifting his lines to meet this disastrous emergency. Duke Blake, he knew, could alternate at either center or right wing. Maybe Duke would do better if spotted somewhere away from Harrigan, who seemed to have his number.

"It's up to you, Duke," he said. "Go out there on the wing."

Duke Blake was tingling with excitement as he skated to his new position. Back on the ice again, back where he belonged.

The Mohawk left-winger, Lennon, had great speed and a vicious shot, but he wasn't as tricky as Harrigan. Duke did a good job of covering him.

The game went on, and Kendall drew a breath of relief as he saw that the switch was working out all right. And when he sent out another line a little later, he put his third-string center into Duke's old spot. This rookie, young and full of fight, was fast enough to cover Harrigan like a blanket.

The period reached the halfway mark, then fifteen minutes, with the score still tied and the teams weary from their efforts to break the deadlock. McMunn and his line went out again.

The Mohawks broke through on the attack. The Flyer goalie saved two close shots, then drilled a long pass to the blue line. McMunn was on it like a flash, wheeled and streaked away.

Duke Blake was with him across the line; Lennon was stranded back in Flyer territory. Down they went on a mad rush, while the crowd rose to its feet and yelled, smelling a goal.

McMunn darted in on the defense, pulled his man over and laid across a pass. Duke snapped it up. McMunn drove through the hole in the defense.

Duke was coming in at an angle. The left defense lunged at him and missed. Duke was through, It was set-up for a goal: hold his shot, pull the goalie out, and pass to McMunn.

But Duke wanted that goal. The winning goal, in front of the Flyer fans, right there on his stick. Why hand McMunn another scoring point and give him a little more glory? Duke weaved in. If he couldn't still beat a goalie single-handed — .

All this went through his mind like lightning. He was in close now, McMunn was waiting in the clear, waiting for that pass.

The goalie made his move! He came

out, flat stick ready as Duke shot.

The goalie came plunging out and flopped to the ice. But his big stick had nailed the puck, sending it skimming to the far boards. The frantic roar of the crowd changed its note — changed to a deep groan of disgust and despair.

Over on the players' bench, Kendall hunched himself down, chin on his chest, mouth bitter.

"It was ticketed! A sure goal! One easy pass, and it was as good as in!" he snarled resentfully. "Of all the bonehead plays, from a man who knows better . . . "

The coach called in the line. McMunn's face was white with anger. He said nothing, but it was plain that he was fuming.

That lost golden opportunity seemed to take the steam out of the Flyers. They never seemed to get back to their peak of sustained speed and fury on the attack.

The Mohawks bored in, rocked the Flyers with a series of wicked thrusts and, with the Flyers hanging on and hoping for overtime, tore in with a ganging attack that ripped the defense to tatters. A close shot, players banging at the rebound, another shot, a save — the goalie down in the net—players milling around the cage, pushing and shoving, the puck lying on the line. A Mohawk wing got his stick free, banged wildly at the rubber and it slid into the cage for the winning goal.

The Mohawks were within one game of the championship. Forty-five seconds later, the siren went and settled that fact beyond dispute.

There was gloom in the Flyer dressing room.

"We should have won it," said Kendall quietly.

Over in a corner, McMunn tore off his gloves and flung them savagely to the floor.

"I'll say we should have won it!" he shouted wrathfully. McMunn glared at the bowed figure of Duke Blake, hunched over on the bench as he fumbled with his laces.

Duke knew he had cost the Flyers the game, but he had become so accustomed to Alex's loyalty that it was a shock to find that his crippled brother wasn't happy with his game.

"What's happened to you Duke?" asked Alex. "The Flyers should have taken that game. Your penalty cost them a goal, and it isn't like you to draw penalties."

"Aw, I just crowded Harrigan into the boards. It might have happened to anybody."

"There was no need to rough him up. And that scoring chance you had when you and McMunn were in close in the last period. Why, it was a set-up, Duke. Why didn't you give him the pass?"

"I figured the goalie would expect a pass and I thought I'd cross him up. I figured wrong, that was all."

"Well, I'm sure disappointed. The Flyers had the best of the play all evening. I thought they should have won."

This didn't improve Duke's temper. Nor did it improve his temper when Kendall brought up a youngster from the Flyers' minor league team for the fourth game and shifted his lines around so that Duke was used in a utility capacity for only a few minutes.

The Flyers won that game. They hit their stride early in the first period and knocked out a decisive 4-1 victory that tied up the series and sent the teams into a fifth game on Mohawk ice. McMunn was the big noise of the Flyers' win with a goal and an assist to his credit.

"He's going to be one of the best in the league," said Alex after the game.

"Anybody would think he was the only center who ever lived!" exploded Duke irritably.

"I'd give anything to be in his shoes," sighed Alex as he limped along the street beside his brother.

"You're better out of it. It doesn't get you anything, this hockey racket, I'm tellin' you. I've been through it. Think it's pretty nice to hear the crowd cheering for you, huh? Well, it doesn't mean a thing! The same gang cheering for you today is hollering at the coach to bench you tomorrow.

"When I was going well, you were strutting around with your chest out, proud to be my brother. I turn in a sour game the other night and you start crabbing right away. I didn't expect any better from the fans, but you — ."

Alex turned a distressed face toward his brother. "But Duke, I wasn't knocking. I couldn't say you turned in a good game, because you didn't. You know yourself . . . "

"I know you've let me down. I thought there was one person in the world I could depend on to pull for me."

"I'm always pulling for you, Duke," answered Alex hotly. "But I'm not going to try to kid you into thinking you're as good as you ever were. The trouble is you won't admit it. Nobody lasts forever in hockey. But you're jealous of McMunn . . . "

"Listen!" snapped the Duke in an ugly voice. "That's enough from you! I don't want to hear another peep."

"Aw, Duke, I'm sorry. I didn't mean to make you sore."

"Shut up!"

It was the first time the brothers had quarreled. And when Duke caught the Flyers' plane that night, he carried with him the recollection of Alex's pale, anxious face.

He had been too proud to square matters with Alex before leaving. Now, on the flight, he had plenty of time for some heavy thinking, and he couldn't escape the stinging jabs of remorse.

The Mohawks' home city was hockey-crazy. The big arena was a complete sell-out. Fans stood in line for hours in the spring rain that splattered on the pavement, stood in line hoping to be lucky enough to get the rush-seat or standing-room tickets that went on sale before game time.

That one game would settle it. The championship was the stake. The Mohawks, with the advantage of playing on home ice with the home crowd behind them, were favored to win.

Duke Blake sniffed like an old war horse when he skated out with the team for the warmup before the game. The arena was jammed to the roof; the noise of the crowd was like the droning of a giant hive. The air was warm, the ice sticky.

Duke took his shots and batted the puck around with the other players. He hoped Kendall would use him tonight. He skated over near the boards. Then he heard an urgent voice shouting:

"Hey, Duke! Duke Blake, look over here!"

He glanced up. A stout, red-faced man was standing up, pounding the rail, beaming at him.

For a moment, Duke didn't recognize this plump, respectable citizen in glasses. And then, he let out a whoop and grabbed the outstretched hand.

"Paddy Gillespie!" he shouted gleefully. "It's been fifteen years since I've seen you."

Paddy was pounding his shoulder. "And isn't it good to see you, Duke. I travelled a long way to see this game. Haven't laid eyes on you since my last pro game, remember? Gosh, that seems a long time ago!"

"You went West, didn't you, Paddy?"

"Yeah, I'm in business out in California. I happened to be East, so I grabbed the chance to come here and see a game again. Gosh, the old Flyer team is changed all to pieces, Duke. You're the only one of the old guard left."

"I'm still sticking around. Gosh, I was only a kid breaking in when you left the Flyers," said Duke.

"You've made a bigger name for yourself than I did when I was playing center for the team. I always knew you were good, Duke."

"You were mighty good to me when I was breaking in, Paddy. Some of the old-timers used to be pretty tough with the rookies."

"Well!" said Paddy Gillespie, "the way I used to figure it, Duke, a fellow has to hang up his skates some time and he might as well do it gracefully. What the heck! I'd had my share. It was your turn. The old-timer has to give way to the rookie, and then the rookie does his stuff for a few years and he steps aside for somebody else. That's the way it goes. Every dog has his day."

Duke looked at him strangely. "Yes," he said, "every dog has his day." Duke could scarcely recognize the burly "Paddy" Gillespie, veteran star of pro hockey's rough-and-ready days. The great Paddy Gillespie, who had been so kind to him when he broke in as a raw rookie with the Flyers!

"The way I used to figure it, Duke," the old-timer was saying, "is that the game is bigger than the player. Some of the veterans used to make it tough for the rookies, trying to hang onto their jobs come hell or high water. But they didn't do their teams any good by it and time always caught up with them in the long run. Hockey comes first, Duke. The player comes second!"

"You're right, Paddy." The team was skating off now; the ice was about to be resurfaced. "Look me up after the game and we'll have a talk."

"Sure thing!"

Duke Blake sat on the bench as the game got under way and stared at the ice with unseeing eyes. He was thinking — thinking of the days when he had first joined the Flyers, and how Paddy Gillespie, whose job at center he had threatened, was kind to him and helped him along.

Duke began to see things from the other fellow's point of view. He had been going around with a chip on his shoulder, letting jealousy and selfishness control him, thinking of himself instead of the team and the game. Nobody was against him—nobody but Old Father Time, and you couldn't lick that old boy.

The lines were being changed. Duke glanced anxiously at Kendall, but the coach ignored him. A second line was going out, with young Dufresne at center opposing Harrigan. A thin, black-haired youngster, the Dufresne kid, just up from the minors, was getting his big chance.

Dufresne stuck to Harrigan like a leech. Harrigan, too, was trying to make good, working his head off in front of a cheering home crowd. He tried rush after rush. But Dufresne clung to him doggedly, covered him relentlessly.

Neither team was taking chances. The checking was close and hard, everybody tense and watchful, waiting for a break. The first period was scoreless. But early in the second came disaster with a penalty for tripping, and the Flyers were left shorthanded.

The Mohawks grabbed the advantage and came storming in when play resumed. A fierce battle inside the Flyer blue line, and, with the goalie sprawled outside the crease after making three quick saves, a rolling, dribbling puck slithered across the line and came to rest just inside the cage.

A thunderous roar seemed to shake the big arena to its very foundations.

Mohawks 1, Flyers 0.

Lines were changed again when the defenseman returned to the ice. Dufresne was out there once more, covering the flashy Harrigan. But the Mohawks were drawing back into their shell, letting the Flyers carry the play to them. Dufresne snared the puck at center ice when he intercepted a pass. He wheeled and broke quickly, outwitted Harrigan, and went flashing in toward the Mohawk defense zone.

Dufresne zipped a pass across to his left wing and ducked toward a hole in the defense. Duke Blake, watching, clenched his hands and rose halfway from his seat. He knew what was coming. Dufresne would never make it. Never.

The two defensemen nailed the rookie in a check that sent him hurtling to the ice. The shot from the incoming wing was blocked and cleared outside. Dufresne lay limp on the frozen surface. The whistle blew, and he was carried off the ice.

"Out you go, Duke" said Kendall unemotionally.

The Duke leaped over the boards and skated up to face Harrigan again as the teams squared away.

If ever Duke Blake was tempted to abandon caution and turn on the heat in a wild effort to do his stuff and tie up the score — it was now! His last game in all probability; his last chance to send the name of Duke Blake singing over the airwaves!

But, as he faced Harrigan, his mouth was tight and grim, his eyes narrowed. The game came first. His job was to hold Harrigan.

He checked Harrigan to a standstill. Harrigan, in frustration tried to get the Duke's goat.

"This is the best break we've had all night," sneered Harrigan. "You lost two games for them already, grandpa. Kendall must be crazy, taking another chance on you."

Skating backward, Duke's stick lashed out and he knocked the puck away from Harrigan's blade, stepped in, and shouldered the other player aside as he batted the disc across to the wing.

"Just about all washed up, Blake?" taunted Harrigan a little later, when they clashed against the boards.

Duke just grinned and held his temper. He had tried the same trick himself in the old days, and had taunted a veteran into a blind rage that earned him a costly penalty. No penalties for Duke to-night!

Toward the end of the second period, when McMunn's line had hurled itself repeatedly against the Mohawk outfit and retired, bruised and discouraged by the solid defense arrayed against them, the Mohawks suddenly came to life and hit back.

They hit back with a smashing counterattack that sent the Flyer players reeling, backed them in behind the blue line and momentarily disorganized them.

There was a wild melee as the Mohawks swarmed in. The Flyer goalie just managed to grab a hard angle shot, kicked out a back-hander that was headed for the lower corner, and smothered the rebound.

The crowd was screeching as the Mohawks put on their ganging act. The goalie went down in the net, lost his stick, crouched there on his knees, trying to stave off flying rubber with his hands.

The puck skittered out of the scrimmage and landed right in front of McMunn. One clear swing at it and the puck would have gone far up the ice and given the Flyers time to get set. McMunn banged it frantically — and missed!

A Mohawk forward swooped in fast. Stick smacked against hard rubber, and the puck sailed straight and true, not three inches off the ice, hard to the twine at the back of the cage, while the crowd went wild with joy, hurled hats, programs, scarfs and pennies to the ice below.

Two goals up, and only a period left to go. A few moments later, the buzzer went, and the disheartened Flyers trooped off the ice.

McMunn was miserable. He crouched on a bench, his head in his hands. Duke Blake sat down beside him.

"Another period yet, kid," he said cheerfully. "We'll take them."

McMunn looked up. "If I hadn't missed that loose puck . . ."

"Aw, forget it! We all miss 'em. Just one of the breaks. We can take this gang."

Duke was the only encouraging and confident player in the dressing room. The rookies on the squad looked at him respectfully, a little brighter now. After all, Duke had seen plenty of hockey. He was bolstering up their courage, giving them new heart.

"If I had a dollar for every game I've seen won in the last period, I'd be worth plenty," he said. "They're tired, I'm telling you. We've got more young players. We can stand it better. We'll be burning up the ice this period when they're just about ready to keel over. See if I'm wrong!"

Kendall was almost goggle-eyed. Duke Blake actually giving the rookies a hand! And they were eating it up. McMunn had a new look in his eyes. The others began squaring their shoulders.

"How's Dufresne?"

"I'm okay now, Duke."

"You were doing a swell job hanging onto Harrigan. We don't need to be afraid of that line while you're out there."

They went on for the third period. And if the Flyers thought they were fighting for a lost cause, they didn't look it. They waded right into the Mohawks.

It was young Dufresne who finally put the Flyers on the score sheet after seven minutes when he stole the puck from Harrigan at center ice, swooped in fast, pulled a defenseman over between himself and the goal, and let fly with a blistering screened shot that slid between the goalie and the post.

The Mohawks tightened up, hanging grimly to that one-goal lead. The Flyers attacked again and again, wearing themselves out against the hard checking.

Fifteen minutes slipped past, and both teams were tired. Five hard games and the end of the long season's trail only a few minutes away!

McMunn was slouched over on the bench, drawing deep, long breaths. He had given everything he had, skated himself into a state of exhaustion, and it had been to no avail. Duke leaned over toward Kendall.

"Coach," he said quietly, "I've got one good goal left in me before I hang up the skates."

Kendall looked him straight in the eyes. What he saw there must have satisfied him. "Go in there on the wing, Duke," he said. "Okay, McMunn. Out there at the next face-off."

It came in a moment. As they skated to their positions. Duke slapped McMunn across the shoulders.

"You've turned in a great game in a tough series. I've got a hunch you're going to win it for us."

McMunn seemed to shake off some of his weariness. "Let's go, Duke!"

Paddy Gillespie — the old-timer who had known Duke when he was breaking into hockey and who said he would have travelled twenty thousand miles to see him at the finish — always said there was nothing in hockey to compare with that last five minutes.

"There he was, you understand," Paddy would say later. "The old Duke, playin' his last game and everybody knew it. And old has-been, see! All washed up. Boys, I'm here to tell you it was as if Duke just dug back into the past and grabbed himself one last handful of all the stickhandling and trickery that had made him one of the greatest players of all time, and flung it into that game."

It was true. For those few minutes, the crowd saw the old Duke Blake out there, drawing on every last resource of his soul and body to give all he had to the game and the team he loved. They saw the same Duke Blake who had sent crowds into frenzy in his great days.

They saw him checking, blocking, stick-handling like a wizard, storming in with McMunn on wild, crashing rushes that sent the leg-weary Mohawks frantically to cover. They saw the Mohawks golfing the puck desperately down the ice to gain time.

And then, they saw Duke Blake go back and pick up the puck inside his own blue line. They saw him go around the net and skate up the right lane pushing the disk ahead of him. They saw him glance out of the corner of his eyes, right and left, barely turning his head. They saw the Mohawk left-winger come out to meet him, the stick lash out.

They saw Duke break sharply; they saw an odd little half step, and then — Duke was flying. Down he came on that quick, darting, zigzag flight, with that swooping, bewildering dash as he hit top speed and stormed down on the defense, streaking through at a blinding pace.

"The old rush! The old Duke Blake rush!" choked Paddy Gillespie, with tears of joy in his eyes.

The defense was pulled over, the goalie was crouching and Duke's stick swung. The goalie plunged for the corner and realized too late he had fallen for a fake shot.

The puck zipped across to McMunn, surging down toward the crease, and then he batted it into the cage. Old Paddy Gillespie hurled a new hat far out on the ice and sent his scarf after it. He whooped like a maniac.

And a little later, with the great minute hand of the clock ticking off the time, they saw young McMunn lead another rush against the shocked and dazed Mohawks.

They saw McMunn, inspired as if new strength had been given him, stick-handle his way down the center and pass to Duke.

They saw Duke and McMunn work their way through the defense and swoop right in on the goal.

Duke Blake was very tired now. He had given everything he had. His knees seemed ready to buckle under him. His arms were heavy, his stick felt like an iron weight. He shoved the puck across to McMunn, and the younger man let drive.

The puck hit the goalie's pads and bounced back. The goalie lunged, tried to smother it and fell sprawling on the ice, outside his crease. McMunn hooked the puck back.

He had nothing to do now but rifle the disk over the prostrate goalie for the winning score; the goal that would give the Flyers the title.

And then, McMunn, in the flash of a second, did something very fine.

"Take it, Duke!" he shouted and pushed the puck across to the veteran.

Duke Blake batted the disk into the open net. And as the light flashed, and the Mohawk crowd groaned with disappointment, and the Flyers flung their sticks in the air, while Paddy Gillespie trumpeted his joy, Duke Blake and McMunn skated back down the ice pounding each other on the back.

A minute later, the buzzer sounded. Duke heard it with a smile. It was the finale of his hockey career, and he was well content.

"See you in a few minutes," he told the wild-eyed Gillespie at the boards. "I want to call up my kid brother long distance."

---- * ----

Emile Francis, coach of the Rangers, wears traditional clothes and believes in short hair. Derek Sanderson is just the opposite. When asked about a possible conflict between his style and that of his coach, Derek said: "No problem. The Cat is gradually coming around. Not long ago he wore a striped shirt to a game. I told him it looked sharp. Now if he'll just grow a mustache I'll go out and buy him some platform shoes."

At the turn of the century, it was quite common for popular players to be presented with a bouquet of roses or violets during a hockey game.

Former NHL referee Red Storey vividly recalls a lady fan who abused him verbally during a hockey game played many years ago . . . during the Second World War.

During a lull in the play, she screamed at him, "Storey, why aren't you in the army?"

And Red quickly replied, "For the same reason you ain't in the Folies Bergères, lady . . . physically unfit!"

Phil Esposito's Wild Ride Through Boston in a Hospital Bed

You should hear Phil Esposito tell the story of his dramatic escape from a hospital in Boston. It's a true story and it happened a couple of years ago after the Boston Bruins were eliminated from the Stanley Cup semi finals by the New York Rangers.

Esposito was injured in the Ranger series and was whisked into hospital where his leg was placed in traction. It wasn't long, of course, before he had visitors. Bobby Orr stopped around with Dallas Smith and one or two other Bruins.

"We're having a windup party tonight, Phil, and you're going to be there," said Bobby.

"No way," said Phil. "The doctors tell me I'll be in here for a few more days. Tell the boys to have a good time at the party. I'll be thinking of them."

"All right, Phil, we'll see you later," said Smith.

And see him later they did. Just after the dinner hour that night, a squad of Bruins paid Phil another visit. This time they came prepared. Two paid volunteers, posing as policemen, distracted the nurses on duty with inquiries about a patient who reportedly had been riddled with bullets. The nurses had no record of such a patient but went scurrying about looking for him.

Meanwhile, the service elevator operator brought Bobby Orr and Dallas Smith up to Esposito's floor. Esposito, still in bed, wearing only his hospital gown and with his leg in traction, was wheeled out of his room and into the elevator. Down on the main floor, the conspirators encountered an obstacle. Espo's bed would not pass through the service entrance because of a metal railing. The players quickly grasped the railing and heaved it aside.

Outside the hospital, no getaway car waited. None could have accommodated the hospital bed and its famous patient anyway.

So the Bruins wheeled Esposito down the main street to the party a few blocks away. Along the way, cars stopped, people gaped. Someone shouted, "There goes Orr! And isn't that Esposito in the bed?"

Phil recalls Bobby Orr instructing him en route, "Left turn, Phil! Quick! Put out your left arm to signal!" Esposito did so as the hospital bed, tires squealing, lurched around a corner.

Safely arriving at the party, Esposito was the guest of honor. Teammates poured him "a little refreshment" to fortify him for the return journey.

Party over, Esposito was returned to the hospital where nurses, doctors, and staff were milling about, frantically trying to track down the absent centerman. Espo quickly fell asleep while his impish teammates were admonished never to pull such a prank again.

The bill for the damaged railing came to $400. Orr, Smith and the other Bruins involved were willing to chip in and cover it but when they discovered Esposito had already paid the bill, they laughed and said, "Tough rocks, Phil. Next time pick a narrower bed when you go joy-riding."

Ken Dryden won't let this shot get past him!

GOALIES ARE DIFFERENT

Look closely at the goalie on your team. Does he act a little strange? Does he surprise you with the things he says and does? If so, don't worry about it. Goaltenders traditionally behave quite unlike the other members of the team.

If you are a goaltender yourself, then you'll know what I mean.

Take the big league goalies. Many of them live in a world all their own. Jacques Plante, early in his career, used to knit toques which he'd wear during a game. Plante later pioneered the regular use of the face mask. He also became the first goalie to wander far out of his net. One time he looked at the goal he was defending and decided it had been measured improperly. The posts appeared to be too far apart. Team officials thought he'd lost his senses when he demanded a measurement. But Plante was right. The distance between the pipes was an inch or so beyond the regulation six feet and new goals were hastily put in play

As he moved from team to team, Plante was also very much a "loner" who lived by himself and did all his own cooking. He's the goalie who explained his job by saying: "How would you like it if you were working in your office and you made one little mistake. Suddenly, a red light went on behind your desk and 17,000 people started screaming at you, calling you a bum and an imbecile. Well, that's what it's like when you play goal in the NHL."

Another goalie, Gump Worsley, was famous in the fifties for daily feuds with his coach, Phil Watson. Watson was forever accusing Worsley of having a beer belly. "You drink too much beer, Gump," was an oft-repeated Watson charge.

"You're crazy, coach," was the inevitable reply. "You know I'm a whiskey man."

When the sniping from Watson became too much for Worsley to bear, he'd snarl, "Keep, talking, coach. I'll be playing in this league long after you're gone." And he was, too.

One time in the fifties the Rangers went on a European tour. Worsley noticed that one of the cities on the tour was Paris, France. He turned to Watson and said, "Coach, when we get to Paris and play that game, if anybody winds up and hits me in the belly with a slapshot the burgundy's going to spurt right out my ears."

Goalies are different, all right.

Former Red Wing star Bob Goldham recalls rooming with a goalie who would go two and three weeks at a time ... without speaking to anybody. He would simply clam up and not say a word.

Glen Hall, who starred with Detroit, Chicago and St. Louis was so nervous

75

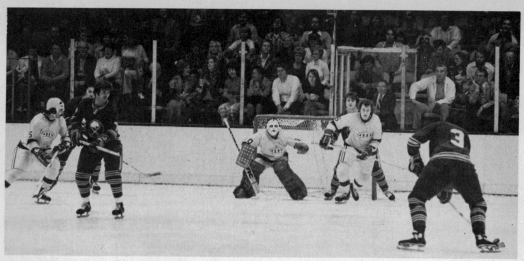

Rogie Vachon faces a Sabre attack.

before every game that he'd throw up. He'd often throw up between periods too.

"It just didn't make sense to feed him on the day of a game," said his wife.

When Bernie Parent jumped from the NHL to the Miami Screaming Eagles of the WHA, who later became the Philadelphia Blazers, he wore jersey number 00 — a hockey first. Later, after jumping across town to the Philadelphia Flyers, Bernie hid his tensions behind his face mask, refusing to doff the mask until he'd reached the privacy of the Flyer dressing room.

"That way," explains Parent, "nobody sees the strain on my face."

Goalies are different because stopping pucks at 120 miles an hour is a nerve-wracking job. Some goalies, sound asleep on a flight between distant cities, will suddenly kick out a leg or wave a catching hand in the air. They're stopping shots . . . in their dreams.

If goalies weren't different, why would Doug Favell eat pizza for breakfast and play professional lacrosse in the off-season, knowing full well a serious injury might end his hockey career? Why would Ken Dryden quit a job at $80,000 a year to work for $135 a week with a Toronto law firm . . . and play hockey *as a defenseman* in an Industrial league? Why would Garry Smith, at a Vancouver press conference called to introduce him to the media announce, "Everything you've heard about me is true . . . I'm a tremendous goaltender!"

Like other goalies, Smith has a burning ambition to score a goal someday. No goalie in the NHL has ever scored. When he was younger, Smith would give his mates and his coach heart failure with mad rushes up the ice with the puck. Except for Smith, few people cared when the NHL introduced a rule forbidding goaltenders from crossing center ice.

Gerry Cheevers is a typical goaltender . . . different. He paints stitches on his mask . . . in the place the stitches would be on his face or head if he hadn't been wearing the mask. That's different.

With Boston one night, Cheevers and the Bruins were blitzed 10-2 by Chicago. Hap Emms, the new Bruin manager, was furious. He stormed into the room after the game and confronted his goalie. "Gerry," he ranted. "What the heck happened out there tonight?"

Cheevers looked up and said, "Very simple, Hap. Roses are red. Violets are blue. They got ten and we got two."

Goalies have always been different.

When the legendary Georges Vezina started out, he much preferred to play

76

Gump Worsley always enjoyed chatting with rival players.

goal wearing street shoes. In fact, he didn't even learn how to skate until he was well into his teens. And any man who fathers 22 children and earns the nickname "Chicoutimi Cucumber" has to be cut from a unique hockey mold.

Most goalies yearn for the day the big league beckons. Not so goalie Johnny Bower. At age 33, playing in Cleveland, Bower's contract was purchased by Toronto. Instead of racing for the next plane to Toronto, Bower said he'd rather stay where he was. He liked it in Cleveland. Didn't want to leave. It took some powerful persuasion by the Leafs to get him to change his mind. In Toronto, he helped the Leafs to win four Stanley Cups. Another Bower trait, common among goalies: he hated to see the puck cross his goal line, and even in practice John became incensed if his teammates scored too often.

Goalie Wilf Cude was once the backup goaltender for several big league teams. He ended his career in unusual fashion. Cude's nerves were going fast and he wasn't sure how many more flying pucks he could face.

On what turned out to be his last day as a big-leaguer, Cude prepared for the game that night. He took his pre-game nap while his wife cooked him a juicy steak. She also cooked one for herself. Called to eat, Cude sat down opposite his wife. He raised his knife when he noticed the table jiggling. He stopped and waited. The jiggling stopped. He raised his knife again and the table jiggled once more. He glanced up. Every time his wife cut into her steak the table shook.

"For some reason," Cude would say later, "that jiggling table sent me into a frenzy. I exploded! I grabbed my steak and heaved it. Threw it right up there on the kitchen wall, sauce and all. And there it hung. Then, slowly, it slipped to the floor. My wife sat there with her mouth open as I grabbed my coat and stormed out the door. I jumped in my car and drove recklessly through the streets, then out into the country. Gradually I cooled off and slowed down and then it was time to go to the arena. But I knew right then I'd never play hockey in the NHL again. Never did, either."

So when somebody tells you goalies are different, don't argue. Most of them are.

MIKE AND PETE GET SPECIAL ATTENTION

Mike Marson is a forward with the Washington Capitals in the NHL. Peter Blair is a potent scorer with the St. Lawrence University hockey club in Canton, N.Y.

Both players are Canadian — Mike from Scarborough, Ontario, and Peter from Ottawa — and both get special attention from opponents and fans alike. The opponents watch them because they are both good; fast and dangerous around the net and improving all the time. The extra attention by the fans stems from the fact that both players are black, a rarity in hockey. They are curious to know if this situation leads to additional pressure on the pair.

"Not really," says Mike. "On the ice, the only problems I have are the same problems facing any young player in the NHL. I'm too busy trying to improve my skills to worry about the race thing. It's never come up. Remember, the guys,

Mike Marson of the Washington Capitols

I'm in with are pros. They won't lower themselves to stupid things like that."

A few month ago, at age 18, Mike was drafted from the Sudbury juniors where he scored 35 goals and 94 points in his only season of junior competition. He earned a reputation in junior hockey as a scrapper but in the NHL he has seldom dropped the gloves. Midway through his rookie season in Washington, he was challenged by the Flyers' tough guy, Don Saleski. Marson nailed Saleski with three or four good punches and was clearly the winner.

Despite the poor record of the Washington entry, Mike had a chance at

Peter Blair—U.S. college star

78

a 20-goal season at the time this was written.

As a U.S. college player, Peter Blair gets less publicity than Mike. But he's no less dedicated.

"I want to play this game to the best of my ability," states Peter. "And I hope to play it at pro level after graduation."

Peter's hard work on the ice is matched by his efforts in the classroom. A popular student, a college degree is at the top of his priority list.

While other black hockey players have performed at the college level, only one has preceded Mike Marson in the NHL ranks. He was Willie O'Ree who played with the Boston Bruins 1959-1961.

```
E  G  R  E  Y  O  N  R  U  O  C  H
W  T  S  E  M  D  R  A  V  A  S  C
O  O  L  R  I  C  H  A  R  D  I  A
H  R  R  U  N  O  S  R  A  M  L  E
A  O  M  S  A  B  R  T  D  T  O  L
E  N  Y  L  L  E  K  N  A  U  P  N
E  T  K  E  T  E  R  E  S  C  H  A
M  O  M  A  O  H  Y  R  W  A  D  H
P  L  A  N  T  E  A  A  E  O  V  E
B  L  A  K  E  L  V  P  R  P  T  E
U  A  E  V  I  L  E  B  I  K  A  M
S  T  R  E  A  G  R  E  V  R  E  V
```

Here's an NHL word puzzle. In it are secret words which you find by solving the clues given below. Remember, the words can run in any direction, up, down, across, backwards, or from the bottom. So be careful. The answers can be found in the back of the book.

1. Center of French Connection Line
2. Wayne & Chico
3. Speedy Montreal R.W.
4. Vanc. R.W. Dennis
5. Toronto Turk in 40's
6. Now plays with sons in W.H.A.
7. Coach of Montreal won 5 Stanley Cups in a row
8. The Gumper
9. Boston's allstar defenseman
10. Great ex-Montreal center
11. Only black player in N.H.L.
12. Ranger L.W. via Pittsburgh
13. Toronto center Dave
14. 4 second demon to the Flyers
15. Boston center and also Montreal defenseman
16. Phila. Vezina winning goalie
17. N.Y. Islander backup goalie
18. Team that won Stanley Cup in 66-67
19. Both Bob's play for Penns. NHL teams
20. Great innovator in goaltending
21. Flyer who took Flett's place
22. Atlanta L.W. Jacques

Meet My Pal
PETER PUCK

BY BRIAN MCFARLANE

Who's the greatest star in hockey? Bobby Orr, you say? Phil Esposito? Gordie Howe?

Would you believe Peter Puck?

Look at the record. In the past couple of seasons, ever since he made his debut on the NHL telecasts, Peter Puck has scored more goals than all the other great shooters combined. It's true the player who whacks him in the net gets credit for the goal, but it's Peter who *actually* does the scoring. At both ends of the rink, too.

I'm convinced Peter Puck is the most popular performer in hockey. And I'm pleased to be called his closest pal.

When Peter made his debut on televised hockey a couple of seasons ago, he asked me to introduce him. Like most performers, he wasn't sure the fans would appreciate his tips on hockey, his simple explanations of rules and regulations. After all, who'd ever heard of a talking hockey puck?

Turned out he had nothing to worry about. Peter was an instant success. In no time, he became the most popular and entertaining intermission guest ever.

Then his fan mail began to roll in. Letters by the hundreds . . . by the thousands. There were questions about hockey, requests for autographs and personal appearances and would you

believe even a couple *of marriage proposals*? It's true.

Peter tried his best to reply to the letters but he found it impossible to answer them all. Just when he'd get started on a batch of mail, the hockey men would

A snowman—Peter Puck built by Scott Damello of Franklin, Maine.

80

My Pal, Peter.

The kids love to shake Pete's hockey glove.

Back in the freezer, Pete. (illustration from book *Peter Puck*)

Pete and I talk hockey at Eaton's.

come along and say, "That's enough, Pete. We're going to put you back in the freezer now. Big game tomorrow."

That's the one aspect of Peter's job I know he doesn't like, sitting in the freezer, ahem, cooling his heels. Oh, he doesn't complain too much because he knows it's important that they put him in the freezer before every game. It takes a lot of the bounce out of him. Come to think of it, sitting in that freezer all night would take the bounce out of *anybody*.

When he wasn't in the freezer, Peter was out on the ice playing hockey. So his mail piled up. And that bothered him.

Then Peter hit on a solution. He'd try to answer all the mail at once . . . especially the hockey questions . . . and put the answers in a book. He asked me to help him with the project and I was happy to agree.

But Peter did most of the work. His creators (Hanna-Barbera Productions Inc.) and his publishers (Methuen) ar-

ranged for layout people, artists and editors. I helped Peter type the manuscript (you should have seen Pete try to type with his hockey gloves on) and I assisted him when he had problems with spelling, helping him overcome the big words . . . like i-c-e and g-o-a-l and z-a-p. (Just kidding, Pete. You really spell very well and when you make a mistake, well, you've got your own built-in eraser).

I guess my main job was to hide him from the hockey men, who kept nosing around asking for Pete. We knew what they wanted. Back in the freezer, Pete.

Eventually the book was finished and it turned out to be a big success.

Then some men in Boston decided to form a Peter Puck Fan Club. The Fan club idea spread to Canada where a major department store (Eaton's) jumped on Pete's bandwagon with special promotions involving my pal.

One week Pete and I visited several stores and met hundreds of young fans.

Pete with some of his fans at Hospital for Sick Children, Toronto.

Peter meets Peter Puk, Jr. (left) and Peter Puk, Sr. (right)

The most popular giveaway item was a Peter Puck decal. We handed out thousands of them.

Pete's interest in children was reflected in his desire to visit the Hospital for Sick Children in Toronto. You should have seen the faces light up when Pete met the youngsters there. Pete was challenged by a young patient to one of those push-pull hockey games and I'm afraid Pete lost badly.

Pete has thousands of relatives. All of them play hockey because, well, that's what hockey pucks *do*. But Pete was amazed to discover he had *human* counterparts named Peter Puck.

During his visit to Toronto, Pete ran into two gentlemen at Maple Leaf Gardens and their names were the same as his . . . Peter Puck.

Well, they weren't *exactly* the same. Peter Puk, Sr. is a teacher in the Toronto School system and his son, Peter Puk, Jr. is a fireman.

You can guess what they talked about. Hockey, of course . . . and how in the world the letter "c" disappeared from the name Peter Puk.

Peter loves his job in hockey. He knows they can't start a game without him and even though the players bash him around with all their might he never gets hurt.

He's a busy little guy who's always on the move. Except, of course, when they put him in that darn freezer.

He's the world's greatest hockey star. And he's my pal.

DID YOU KNOW?

That *two* skate sharpening machines are used by most pro clubs. One is a "rougher" machine which cuts out the nicks. The other is then used to make the hollow edge.

Early day goalies wore ordinary shin pads. In 1896, G.H. Merritt, a Winnipeg goalie, began using white cricket pads to protect his shins and the style was soon copied by all goalies.

Around the turn of the century, most "boards" surrounding hockey rinks were only a foot high. Spectators had to be ready to leap out of the way of flying pucks.

In 1898, the goalie for Ottawa, Fred Chittick, refused to play because the team manager would not allot him a number of complimentary tickets to home games.

In 1903, a Winnipeg team startled hockey fans by wearing long dressing gowns in the pre-game workout, presumably to keep warm.

When Rat Portage (Kenora) challenged Ottawa for the Stanley Cup in 1903 only one player on the Rat Portage team had reached the age of 21.

Was it murder on ice? In 1907, Owen McCourt of Cornwall died in hospital after being struck over the head with a hockey stick. A rival player, Charles Masson of Ottawa, was charged with murder, a charge later reduced to one of manslaughter. At the trial, witnesses mentioned the possibility of another player's stick dealing the blow and Masson was acquitted.

GARRY HOWATT

MILTON RICHMAN

New York (UPI) — Tony "Poosh 'Em Up" Lazzeri never talked about it. He felt there was so much ignorance and prejudice on the part of people about the subject that it was better they didn't know of his affliction.

Tony Lazzeri played second base 12 years for the New York Yankees, handling the position as if he was born there, and he was part of murderers' row, yet only the closest to him knew he was an epileptic.

So was Grover Cleveland Alexander, who struck him out with the bases full in the 1926 World Series.

There is still a great deal of ignorance about epilepsy today.

What is known is that it is a disorder of the nervous system which comes in three types: grand mal, petit mal, and psychic equivalent to psychomotor attacks. Also known is that males are more commonly affected than females and most cases begin in childhood or adolescence.

That was when it all started for Garry (Toy Tiger) Howatt, who's playing such a bang-up game now for the New York Islanders of the NHL and isn't the least bit self-conscious about discussing his condition.

"I remember the first time I ever had a seizure. I was 14 years old," say the Islanders' stocky 22-year-old left winger.

"I was sick that day and didn't go to

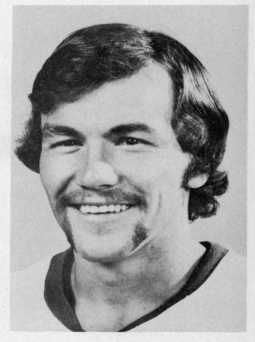

school. I was lying on the couch with a bad headache and bad feeling in my stomach and I remember my dad coming in from doing the chores. Oh, Jeez, it was really weird. I didn't know what it was, but I knew it was bad. I was frightened. The whole thing lasted about 10 minutes. I got sick, very sick all over afterwards."

Epilepsy often is accompanied by a convulsion in which the victim falls involuntarily. Garry Howatt remembers falling out of bed and hitting his head on the floor when he was 17 and that was the last time he had a seizure.

His condition is controlled and the way he controls it is by taking a mysoline pill three times a day and phenobarbital pill once a day.

If you've ever seen Garry Howatt perform with the Islanders then you know his condition doesn't handicap him a bit. He's always aggressive, ready to go anytime. They call him the "Toy Tiger" because at 5'9" and 170 he takes on all comers in the League and one of the decisions he owns is over Philadelphia's celebrated bad boy, Dave Schultz.

"I feel I'm just as fit as anybody else," says Howatt, who led the league with 30 major penalties in 1973-74. This year he's concentrating more on scoring.

Due to some of the ignorance about epilepsy and the fact doctors didn't really control it until a relatively short time ago, some victims still have trouble finding jobs. Doctors have advised epileptic patients to keep their condition from their employers because of the prejudice which still exists to some degree.

Garry Howatt doesn't go around broadcasting his condition, but neither does he make any secret of it.

When he was getting his first medical checkup with the Islanders, he voluntarily told the doctors what he had and asked them whether it would affect his playing. They said no — providing he kept the disorder under control.

"I used to get down a lot when I was younger," says Howatt, who comes from Grand Center, Alberta. "I used to wonder whether my condition would keep me from playing hockey. My mom and dad always encouraged me. They told me to keep working hard."

Howatt did that.

He doesn't have all the talent and finesse in the world out on the ice, but when it comes to working hard, digging in and giving it everything he's got, Garry Howatt is right up there with the best of them. Maybe even a little ahead.

In a game last season, the Canadiens were leading Rangers 7-1 after two periods of play.

One of the Habs urged his teammates not to let up. "Remember the Detroit game," he said. "We led 3-1 and they came back to beat us."

"That's right," agreed several mates.

"I remember a game in Toronto," said Bob Gainey quietly. "The Leafs were beating Rangers 7-1 after two periods."

"So. What happened?" asked Pete Mahovlich.

"Nothing. Toronto went on to win 9-1," grinned Gainey.

Marty Howe: On his father and teammate, Gordie: "He's built like no one else in the world. His arms begin at his ears."

Dave Schultz is Hockey's exorcist . . . He scares the devil out of you.

The first artificial ice rink was opened in London, England in 1876.

The first recorded hockey game in Canada was played in Montreal on a Saturday afternoon in February of 1835.

In January of 1903 The Winnipeg Victorias iced a hockey team all wearing tube skates. Tube skates were worn as early as 1900 by Jack Marshall of Winnipeg.

In 1909 Ottawa played a game against Cobalt with the temperature 21 below zero. Only a handful of people turned out and the goal judges retired after 20 minutes with frozen feet and noses.

Jackie Hamilton and Red Storey

How Long Can A Fellow Play This Game, Anyway?

"If you love the game of hockey," states Jackie Hamilton, "you can play forever."

"Well, maybe not that long," he says on second thought. "But you should be able to play until you get so old and fat that you can't bend over to tie up your skate laces anymore."

Hamilton, now fifty years of age, admits he has a little difficulty tying his own skates laces these days.

"I have to cross one leg over the other to get at them now," he admits. "I guess that's because I'm a pound or two over my normal playing weight."

Jackie's comment draws snorts of laughter from his teammates on the NHL Oldtimers. "A pound or two over his normal weight!" roars one. "Make that a hundred pounds over. I remember when Jackie played for the Leafs in the forties. Why, he was just a little runt. Never weighed more than 150 pounds. Look at him now! He steps on the ice now and the scoreboard flashes 'TILT'"

Jackie takes the kidding in stride. The doctors have warned him to slim down and take things easy on the ice. And he'd like to be skinny again . . . but gee . . . it's not all that easy, you know.

Besides, he still moves around that ice like . . . in his words . . . "a phantom."

"Yeah . . . a FAT phantom!" quips a teammate.

"That's it! No more passes for you," is Jackie's reply, as he heads for the ice surface and another Oldtimer's game.

During the game he holds the spotlight, amusing all with his antics. He cavorts down the ice in a spectacular dash, the puck never straying more than a foot from his flashing stick. He scores! Arms and stick upraised, the secret is revealed. The puck is tied to his stick with a short length of twine.

Later, hotly disputing a referee's decision, Jackie chases the official around the rink and wrestles him to the ice. He pulls and tugs on the referee's striped jersey until the trophy is claimed and held aloft. The winded official concedes and Jackie's penalty time is erased from the ledger.

He draws his biggest laugh a few minutes later. He sprawls on the ice, clutching his mammoth stomach. Players from both teams anxiously surround him. The team trainer rushes out, dragging a medical bag. Suddenly, from out of the huddle, undergarments fly through the air. Women's undergarments. Bits of silk, flowered panties, bras and corsets.

Then, assisted to his feet, Jackie fumbles under his jersey and produces a baby! Well, from a distance the rubber doll *looks* like a baby. And the crowd roars as he circles the ice holding the newborn infant aloft between kisses and cuddles.

It may not be much of a comedy routine . . . but when Jackie Hamilton performs the crowd roars its approval.

They've come to enjoy a hockey game, and Jackie Hamilton, big belly concealing a bigger heart, is the Clown Prince of the Geritol set . . . a middle-aged Eddie Shack doing what he does best . . . putting a little fun into the game.

COACHING CORNER

Good Goalies Hug the Post

From time to time you hear hockey commentators talk about goaltenders "hugging the goalpost."

That doesn't mean that goalies embrace the slender red post like it was a sweet young thing with love in her eye. Even goalies aren't that dumb!

In hockey jargon, "hugging the post" means that the smart goalie protects the corner of the net, so that no clever opponent will slip the puck in from behind or beside the net. Goalies know that hockey pucks are only three inches in circumference and one inch thick and that pucks have a nasty habit of finding their way through cracks and openings that often seem to be only a fraction of that size.

Goalies who "hug the post" cut down on any chance (*they hope*) of a puck finding a way into the net if the play develops from in back of the net or from the corner.

Take a look at the photo. Pittsburgh goalie Gary Inness is "hugging the post" in such a manner that it's almost impossible to score from behind or beside the net. He has left only one tiny opening where his right knee is bent and chances are slim a puck will find its way in there. His right arm, or stick hand, is outside the post, holding the stick so that any passout from in back of the net can be deflected away. His body is facing toward the front of the net in case the puck should be flipped in front and he'll be called upon to face a shot from the slot area.

If the puck should go to the opposite corner he's in a good position to slide across the crease and hug the opposite post.

And he's got his eye on the puck at all times. That's playing goal the way it should be played.

A new season is underway. You've got a new coach. Perhaps you're on a new team in a new league. You've got new objectives . . . and new equipment.

To help you obtain the goals you have set for yourself, heed the following advice insofar as equipment is concerned:

Gloves

In selecting a pair of gloves, make certain the thumb area is well protected. The price range for gloves varies considerably. This makes it possible for most players to be properly outfitted, regardless of expense.

Shin Guards

Shin guards, like gloves, need not be expensive to provide adequate protection. Make sure the area just above the top of the skate is covered by the shin guard and the guard fits properly over

Pittsburgh Goalie, Gary Inness.

the knee area. Generous flaps on the sides of the guards will protect all but the very back of the leg.

Shoulder Pads

These pads are probably the least essential equipment item in the player's bag. Forwards normally wear lighter weight shoulder pads than defensemen. Avoid cumbersome, bulky pads that restrict the natural motion of the arms and shoulders.

Skates

The most important part of your equipment, old or new, will be your skates. Old skates should be tested early to find out if the fit is still comfortable. New skates should be fitted properly. It is better to purchase a medium-price skate every season than to purchase an expensive skate that a player will "grow into" and last two or three years. When trying on a pair of skates, make sure the heel of the foot is "seated" (*kicked back into place*) and the laces are tied as tightly as possible. The heel should not slip and the lacing should not be too close.

Elbow Pads

A "must" on every player's equipment list. Make sure of a proper fit here. Elbow pads that are too big will slip away from the elbow and injury could easily follow. If you've ever played without elbow pads for a game or two you'll know how often the elbows come in contact with sticks, boards and ice. Ouch!

Helmets

No young player should ever participate in a game or practice without a helmet ... and a tooth protector. Don't skimp here. Take time to select a helmet that will give maximum protection and comfort.

Those are the major equipment items. Choose with care but remember, brand new equipment often strains the family budget. There's nothing wrong in seeking out second-hand or hand-me-down equipment. Often, excellent bargains can be found at skate exchanges and by reading the daily want ads in the local newspaper.

What can a young player learn from the photo of Guy Lapointe? Lapointe has lost his stick and his right glove in a skirmish along the boards. Does he take time to retrieve his stick and glove while the play goes on? Not Guy.

First, he must get back into the play and help his team. He'll worry about his stick and glove later. So he dashes in to protect goaltender Ken Dryden. If a shot comes from the point, Guy is ready to go down to block it. He doesn't need a stick for that. With some luck, he'll be able to smother the shot and force a face-off.

Lapointe protects his goalie even without stick and glove.

Then he'll have time to find his missing equipment.

When young players lose a stick or a glove, they often take precious seconds to make up their minds. Should they scramble after the equipment or get back in the play? It's not *always* better to ignore the missing gear and play without. If the play is in the center ice area and there's little chance of a goal being scored, perhaps it's best to retrieve the stick or glove.

If the play is deep in your own zone, the second or two it takes to recover the equipment may cost your team a goal. That's when you must decide instantly (as Lapointe did) to play as best you can despite the disadvantage.

In The Corners:
You Don't Have Time
To Look Both Ways

As a child, when you first learn to walk, you are taught basic safety rules. Don't play with matches. Stop on the corner. Wait for the green light. Look both ways before crossing the street. All very important reminders.

But in hockey's corners, you don't have time to look both ways. Not always. And there are no lights to tell you when to stop and go. And there's always the danger of getting crunched by what feels like a runaway truck but in reality is only a rather large, mean defenseman. Some Christmas present.

Very few goals are scored from the corners but countless games have been won and lost there. Every team needs good corner men, players who are not afraid to dash in and battle for the pucks that invariably wind up there. Forwards who fail to dig in the corners, fearful they'll be bowled over by opposing defenseman, seldom advance far beyond amateur hockey. It's true that corner play can get rough. Chasing pucks into corners can be one of the least pleasant aspects of hockey, like taking out the garbage at home. One of those things that has to be done even though you feel like taking a deep breath before doing it.

In the corners, take a quick look if possible to see who's coming in behind you. It may enable you to avoid a stiff

Playing the corners takes a special kind of skill. Invariably a winning team has players who can dig the puck out of the corners.

check. And keep moving. Even shifting a few inches may save you from being bodychecked into the boards. Remember, if you don't like going in the corners, neither do most of the other players on the ice, even rival defenseman.

I laughed when I read what Jim McKenney of the Leafs said not long ago.

A reporter asked Jim who gave him the most trouble in the corners.

And Jim answered: "I don't know. I never go in the corners if I can help it."

PEE-WEE AND HIS PALS by Bill Reid

HOCKEY
Questions & Answers

When did the Zamboni ice machines make their appearance and why are they called Zambonis?

The Zamboni ice re-surfacer is the invention of Frank J. Zamboni of Paramount, California. In 1938, Mr. Zamboni owned an ice rink in California and he devised the machine now commonly known as the Zamboni after much research and experimentation. In 1949, the famous figure skater Sonja Henie ordered a machine for use in her ice show and shortly after, many arenas began taking an interest in the Zamboni invention. Now, over a quarter of a century later, close to 1400 Zamboni machines are in regular use all over the world.

How far can a goalie come out of his crease?

A goalie can move out of his crease anywhere in his half of the hockey rink. But if he crosses the center ice red line and participates in the play he will receive a two minute penalty.

Why don't most hockey players wear teeth guards like the prizefighter's do? They might keep their teeth longer if they did.

Right on. Professional players, many of whom have lost some teeth to hockey, often claim that boxer-type teeth guards "hamper their breathing" or "they just don't feel right." The fact is, modern, custom made, comfortable teeth guards are now available and should be worn

One of the earliest Zambonis . . . circa 1949. A very primitive model.

Today's Zamboni. Sleek and streamlined.

by *all* players interested in protecting their teeth. In minor hockey, it is mandatory that all players wear some form of protector for their teeth. It's a great rule.

Let me add a personal note. I never wore a mouth guard when I played hockey as a boy and I had my teeth

95

broken off on one occasion and knocked out on another. I wish they'd had proper tooth protection in those days.

Now that I'm older, I must be getting smarter because I've been wearing a custom-fitting tooth protector for a couple of seasons.

It's comfortable and it's great.

I would like to know how the NHL figures out a goaltender's goals against average.

In determining the goaltender's goals against average, the following method is used. Take the goals against, multiply by 60 and divide by the total minutes played. To simplify it, let's say a goalie plays 2,345 minutes over the season and has 78 goals scored against him. Multiply 78 by 60 and you get 4,680. Then divide 4,680 by 2,345 and you come up with 1.99. Hey, that goalie has a pretty fair average!

Who holds the record for the fastest goal from the start of a game?

On February 19, 1975, Cleveland Crusader Russ Walker scored against the Minnesota Fighting Saints just five seconds after the opening whistle, a professional hockey record. In the NHL,

Henry Boucha, then with Detroit, scored a goal against Montreal after just six seconds of play. That was on January 28, 1973.

Since hockey players get traded around a lot, can you tell me who has belonged to the most number of teams in his career?

Larry Hillman of the Cleveland Crusaders is pro hockey's most-travelled player. Now celebrating 20 years as a pro. Larry has belonged (*on paper*) to 17 teams and actually played for 14. Now 38, Larry says he hopes to play for another couple of years.

When was the first penalty shot taken in the NHL?

The first penalty shot ever taken in the NHL was by a player named Armand Mondou of the Montreal Canadiens. It was awarded in Toronto, on Nov. 10, 1934 against Leaf goalie George Hainsworth. Hainsworth stopped Mondou's shot and the Leafs won 2-1. Three days later, Ralph Bowman of St. Louis became the first player to score on a penalty shot when he beat goalie Alex Connell of the Montreal Maroons in a game played at St. Louis.

PEE-WEE AND HIS PALS *by Bill Reid*

From: The Chicago Tribune Magazine, January 19, 1975.

Keeping Peace Among The ≈ Pros ≈

Linesman Neil Armstrong's job ranges from stalling the action for the sake of a TV commercial to wrestling with snarling athletes. As he says, "You never know who had a dish of raw meat before the game."

BY ROBERT CROSS

He stands tall and self-assured amid that subtle athletic presence in the hotel lobby. Big men in "designer" suits gather in knots, pace by themselves, mill around. They look slightly bored but dangerous too, and they give off just the faintest crackle of tension and suppressed energy.

If this is Saturday, it must be Kansas City, and Neil Armstrong—as tall as the rest, slimmer than most, and more gray-haired—is waiting for this evening when he will have these men under his control.

They are hockey players, members of the Chicago Black Hawks, and Armstrong is a linesman, one of the 44 National Hockey League officials who regulate the games these people play. At work, Armstrong wears a black-and-white striped shirt and carries a whistle. He will divide the ice with another linesman, Bob Hodges, and Referee Dave Newell, neither of whom have come downstairs yet.

Unlike baseball umpires, who work in teams and often stay in one town for a complete home stand, hockey officials are required to float from city to city in endlessly changing combinations.

"We try to avoid overexposure," says Scotty Morrison—their chief supervisor — from his league office in Toronto. "We often say that every time an official makes a decision, he's 50 per cent wrong: one of the clubs won't agree. If an official stayed with a team, even in different cities, they'd be sick and tired of seeing that individual, and the feeling would be mutual. That's the sort of thing we try very hard to avoid."

Travel, then, has become a big part of the job. Armstrong has traveled 9,000 miles in this young season — of the 100,000 or so he will log for the year — and he hasn't seen the Hawks till now. He says hello to a few; they smile. Some might ask after his wife, Marg, and the kids — Lezleigh, 13, and Douglas, 11. They get to see Armstrong approximately every eight days, when Morrison's periodic schedule (issued only a week or so in advance) places the linesman near his hometown on the Canadian side of the St. Clair River.

"You fellas play at least 50 per cent of

97

your games at home," Armstrong likes to point out when he hears an athlete complain about the endless cycle of airports and coffee-shop steaks, "but they haven't had a game in Sarnia, Ontario, yet; *all* my games are on the road."

It's a wonder that the league hasn't franchised a team from Armstrong's hometown. The N.H.L. version of big-league hockey now takes place in 18 cities, and some of them must sound ludicrous to old-time fans. Uniondale, Long Island? Washington, D.C.? (Do the locals there pelt the ice with magnolia and old campaign buttons?) About the only time Sarnia sees a top player is when one of them drops by to visit Armstrong in the off season (he works as the golf pro at the Sarnia Golf and Curling Club); but the way things have been going, we may see the Sarnia Oilers, or something, any time now.

The league calls it "expansion" and the sportswriters call it "dilution", but it certainly isn't anything like those proud days of yore when only six teams fought for the Stanley Cup and the entire roster of officials couldn't fill the counter of a Howard Johnson's.

This night, for example, will mark the home debut of the Kansas City Scouts. But game time is far away. Stomachs in the hotel lobby are growling, and a barely noticeable lunchtime protocol goes into effect. Armstrong has been joking with a Hawk or two, but inside the dining room, the players go their own way, leaving the lineman to wait for his partners in a remote booth.

A few years back, when an official might visit a city perhaps 14 times a season, he was not permitted to use the same lodging as the visiting team. That rule has been relaxed with expansion/dilution, because Scotty Morrison *must* know where his employees are at all times in case he has to shift an assignment. If an official said uh-oh and checked out every time he saw a player in his hotel, Morrison's precise schedule could become a shambles.

Only Tony Esposito, the Hawk goalie,

lingers by Armstrong's booth for a moment. "Whatta ya know, Tony? Good summer?" Armstrong says.

"Pretty good," says Tony. "Howya been?"

"Oh, 60-40, take your choice. Getting by, getting a couple meals a day. So far it's fine. Touch wood." Armstrong raps his knuckles on the tabletop. He has plenty of room at the booth, but he does not ask Esposito to sit down.

"It would be in bad taste," he explains later. "Rules against fraternizing are mostly for the public image. In the summertime, some of the players come into Sarnia and play golf — but never during the season. Tony came over and said hello because I haven't seen him yet this year and we've known each other a long time. But just assume that gentleman sitting over there is a really ardent Kansas City hockey fan. You don't want to give them anything to complain about. Besides, it *is* a league rule."

Those who watch hockey with any regularity might wonder how fraternizing could ever become a problem anyway, so intense is the play and so passionate are the arguments. Linesmen are the ones who separate the fighters during brawls, and these are becoming more frequent. It was only natural; now that dilution prevails, not all the teams can play great hockey, so some of them have added mayhem to the starting lineup. The fans seem to enjoy that. When bloodlust and skill combined in 1973 and the Philadelphia Flyers — a team seemingly bred for savagery—captured the Stanley Cup, their success was sure to increase the incidence of brute force around the league even more.

It has gotten to the point where a linesman cannot look forward to a peaceful game with graceful skating, clean checking, and gentlemanly behavior. If he were to focus entirely on the puck in these treacherous times, he might overlook a shocking dismemberment taking place across the rink. Yet if he *doesn't* watch the puck—well, that's dangerous too.

"On any day, any team can get rough," says Armstrong. "You never know who had a dish of raw meat before the game."

Bob Hodges, the other linesman for this evening, has turned up in Kansas City with a ragged red bruise under his right eye. "I got it in Chicago last Sunday," he explains with a touch of embarrassment. "I was real foggy there for a while."

"A 2-1 hockey game is much better for me to work," says Armstrong. "Everybody has their own job to do. You're bearing down, the players are bearing down. In a 10-3 game, you become a spectator. You're always feeling, 'What the hell's going on? Who did that?' You start watching the player instead of the puck."

Armstrong's understanding, however, doesn't prevent him from poking fun at Hodges. In one of their cab rides today, Armstrong is chortling, "If you're looking for sympathy, go find it in the dictionary." He tells a couple of Scout fans that Hodges sustained his injury "in a girls-school yard." And Hodges, who at 30 is 11 years younger than his partner for this game, finally tells Armstrong, "Don't let it happen to you when I'm workin' with ya, 'cause I'll just laugh!"

In peacetime, the hockey linesman's job has all the excitement of a slow morning at the Lincoln Park lagoon. He ambles down his side of the rink along with the ebb and flow of player traffic, watching for illegal passes, offsides, and "icing". Newell, the referee, must keep an eye out for more serious violations — tripping, elbowing, spearing, or slashing, for instance — that could cost a player some time in the penalty box.

During fights, the referee must watch for even more serious violations, so he stands back while the linesmen move in at great risk of teeth and collarbones (shins and groins, at least as vulnerable, are shielded in high-impact plastic). Yet, before game time, Referee Newell seems far more tense than his colleagues. He speaks hardly at all in the cab, while Armstrong points out a shouting, stumbling old drunk and says, "There's an old referee right there. Give 'em hell, boy!" "A retired *Linesman*," Newell murmurs. They pass a bar that Armstrong discovered last night. "Keep a cool one on tap, boys," he says. "We might be back here later." A car up ahead is a bit slow pulling away from the light, and Armstrong yells, "It's not going to get any greener, you donkey!" Armstrong's exuberance seems to grow as they get closer to the arena. His partners become virtually silent. When things go wrong in a hockey game, N.H.L. executives tend to look to the referee and the younger officials first if there's blame to be handed out. Clarence S. Campbell, the league president, will be in attendance tonight, so the pressure to do well is that much more intense.

Because the linesmen are the ones who start and stop play most often, a Scout official pulls Armstrong aside — instead of Newell — and explains how the TV commercials will be inserted. When play is stopped for an offside or something and a linesman is ready to drop the puck, the television crew will signal Armstrong on a pocket beeper if it's time for a commercial. Then the linesman will stall until another beep tells him the commercial is done.

The game is well fought but, from an official's standpoint, uneventful. No fights. Hawk Coach Billy Reay, whose team eventually wins 4-3, does not choose to start his one annual argument with Armstrong ("You know you're going to have it sometime," Neil says, "it's just a question of when."). The play is close enough to provide that extra edge of concentration. Even the commercials get their due time with the obvious sort of stall that makes fans boo; the ice is chippy, and there is plenty of legitimate reason to delay the game and try to rub out the rough spots.

At one point, that roughness causes

Bob Hodges to fall, and a corner of his wallet takes a nasty dig into the flesh of his upper left thigh.

The game is finished; all three have regained their athletically dapper appearance, and as usual Armstrong is the first to leave their tiny dressing room. Two of the television broadcasters seek him out in the hallway under the stands and thank him. "That was *beautiful*," one says, "the way you got down there and rubbed the ice — great! Some of those guys just stand there staring up at us during commercials." Armstrong nods.

It could have been brutal, of course, and then the linesman would have called upon techniques learned mostly through sad experience. Armstrong now has more games than any other official in the league and he views the combat with disinterest. "Basically, we're paid to officiate the game, not to be peacemakers," he explains softly. "If two players are evenly matched and slugging it out, we might stand back for 30 seconds or so and let them get in two or three good punches. Usually we wait until they fall to the ice or clutch each other. Then I'll say to Bob, or Bob will say to me, 'I've got the red, you take white.' One official will never go into a fight alone. Not because he's afraid; it just makes sense that if I'm hanging on to one person it gives the other guy an advantage."

Armstrong makes it sound cool and polite, but in actual practice, of course, the linesman must disengage a flailing, cursing athlete who's usually devoid of front teeth and looking just that much more fierce. Both linesman and player are wearing skates on almost frictionless ice and trying to stay balanced in their awkward pads. And the player, disconcertingly enough, is usually screaming something like, "Next time I see you I'm gonna take your head off, you_____!!!" Naturally the player's remarks are aimed at his opponent, not the officials. Any abuse directed at an official can be costly for the player and his team. ("He'll get at least 10 minutes

to think about it," Armstrong promises.)

The referee, all the while, keeps his distance, watching for the first player to leave his bench during the melee and keeping track of other infractions—a bit like God in a striped shirt, aloof but all-knowing.

That's about all there is to it. Hockey is a basically simple game, played by men (nearly all of them Canadian) who have been at it almost since they learned to walk. It is not a game in which the personnel dwell on the subject of fear, and most of their faces are pocked with the scars of combat, little white tracks representing stitches taken without anesthetic in the brave sweaty stench of a dressing room.

Armstrong is of that stoic tradition. His boyhood home, Galt, Ontario, seethed with hockey competition, as most Canadian towns do. As a teen-ager, he began to officiate at Pee Wee games for 50 cents apiece. He would sometimes make $2 that way on a busy Saturday and still find time to play on his own team. Then came invitations to work playoffs, and that led to important interprovince competitions and finally to the minor professional leagues.

Neil dropped out of school at the 11th grade and began devoting his winters to hockey and a part-time job in a clothing store. In summer he took employment at country clubs, slowly working his way from the bag room to the lesson tee. Hockey is always viewed with a degree of fatalism by the young men who aspire to its various levels. So few can reach the heights that it's best not to count on anything. So many are stopped short by injuries that it's prudent to think small and avoid disappointment. Armstrong thought he had a good hobby in hockey officiating, but in 1965 he was invited to officiate at an N.H.L. game and, for the first time, felt the shaft of professional ambition: he wanted *so much* to do well in Maple Leaf Gardens, where Toronto would play the Boston Bruins.

And he did do well until just before the end. He cannot remember the score anymore — scorekeepers are paid to do that — but he remembers the weight of the huge crowd, the extraordinary skill of the players, and his intense desire to show his competence. Then, with five minutes to go, a fight began — not one of those fleeting exchanges of punches, but a full-scale riot with both teams clearing their benches and everyone breathing death. "All hell broke loose," Armstrong recalls.

His partner ordered Armstrong to grab somebody, so he came in behind Boston's Ferny Flaman and pulled him out of the brawl. Somehow, Armstrong figures, he and the referee — also a rookie — would be blamed for this chaos. He was already feeling sorry for himself when he suddenly felt Flaman's arm go limp; it hung from its socket, swinging crazily, and Flaman snarled, "Kid, you're in trouble. You broke my arm."

Armstrong just stared. His career had begun — and probably ended — in such utter disaster that he could not even find the words to apologize. Then Flaman laughed and winked, flexing his arm to show that it had been a big joke. "I could have punched him in the nose," Armstrong says now, "but I was too scared."

"This isn't kid stuff you're playing with," Flaman warned him. "You're in the men's league now."

How true. The fans in some cities can make life miserable; coaches and veteran players have refined the art of insult. But referees take the brunt of their wrath, not linesmen. Two seasons ago, the Black Hawks' Bill White was suspended without pay for five games after grabbing Referee Ron Wicks in a moment of rage. Coach Reay, while not condoning White's action, remarked that he thought Wicks had called a "rotten" game. John D'Amico had to resume his duties as a linesman after trying to referee for a while; the pressure was giving him a severe rash. Former Referee Bill Chadwick reportedly chewed his nails so much that his fingers bled all season.

And then we have Armstrong, making about $17,000 a year from hockey alone ("If I had his money, I'd burn mine," says Hodges, who works as a park landscaper in the summer), exuding good cheer, staying on top and loving it there in Macho Heaven. Why be a referee, training down there in the minor leagues at his age? This life is good enough.

In the hotel lobby, long after the game, the three officials are about to search for food in a barren downtown. The only life to speak of is right where they're standing: Stevie Wonder fans, fresh from a rock concert in the auditorium across the street are pouring into the hotel. Stevie himself, enclosed by heavy-duty entourage, is passing through.

"What's going on?" Armstrong asks a woman. "Stevie who? I guess that dates me. I'm too old. Is he any good?" His eyes glow. How else would a smalltown Canadian boy find himself plunged into big-city excitement like this day after day? It's wonderful. And after 18 years, Neil Armstrong is certain that he is very good indeed.

* * ✳ * *

Phil Esposito tells this one:
"After the first Team Canada-Russia hockey series, there was a reception in Moscow for the players. I went over to Alexander Yakushev, one of the greatest left wingers I've ever seen, and I said, 'Alex you come to play in Boston and I'll get you $100,000 a year. What's more, I'll only take 15 per cent as my commission.'
"He listened while the interpreter relayed my offer. Then he broke into a grin and said, 'Phil, you come to play in Moscow with my team, Spartak, and I'll get you a free apartment.'"

HOCKEY QUIZ

Try this multiple choice quiz involving famous hockey "firsts:"

1. The first Stanley Cup game was played in

  1. Montreal 2. Boston
  3. Vancouver 4. Flin Flon

2. The first U.S. team to join the NHL was

  1. Boston 2. New York
  3. Chicago 4. Boise, Idaho

3. The first player to score 50 goals in a single season was

  1. Gordie Howe
  2. Rocket Richard
  3. Eddie Shack
  4. Bobby Orr

4. The NHL was formed in 1917-18. The first NHL city to win the Stanley Cup was

  1. Toronto 2. Montreal
  3. Boston 4. Renfrew

5. The first player to score over 70 goals in a single season was

  1. Bobby Orr 2. Bobby Hull
  3. Phil Esposito
  4. Tony Esposito

6. The first President of the NHL was a man named

  1. Campbell 2. Calder
  3. Dutton 4. Nixon

7. The first black player to play in the NHL was

  1. Jackie Robinson
  2. Mike Marson
  3. Willie O'Ree
  4. Flip Wilson

8. The first coach of the Kansas City Scouts was

  1. Bep Guidolin 2. Sid Abel
  3. Scotty Bowman
  4. Derek Sanderson

9. The first play-by-play announcer of Toronto Maple Leafs games was

  1. Danny Gallivan
  2. Tim Ryan
  3. Foster Hewitt 4. Peter Puck

10. The first Team Canada— Russia series (in 1972) was won by

  1. Russia 2. Canada
  3. Sweden 4. Czechoslavakia

(Answers at the back of the book)

From Trees to Hat Tricks

BY ONIL MERCIER

1. Every Victoriaville hockey stick starts out the same way: as a tree in our northern white ash forests. White ash is selected for all Victoriaville hockey sticks because of its straightness and regularity of the grain.

2. When a supply of white ash arrives at the Victoriaville mill in the Province of Quebec, Canada, it is cut into handle length logs.

3. Powerful saws then strip the bark from each log and cut it into planks.

4. As the planks are planed into shafts, they begin to take on the familiar shape of a hockey stick handle.

5. Meanwhile, blade blanks are being cut to size from smaller white ash logs.

6. Since even white ash isn't uniformly strong and durable, Victoriaville experts inspect and grade every rough shaft and blade blank.

7, 8. After the approved shafts and blade blanks are kiln-dried for toughness, skilled craftsmen join the handle to the blade. Unlike any other sticks, Victoriaville's blades and shafts are welded into a 4-piece joint by way of a hot gluing process under thousands of pounds of pressure for maximum strength in this most critical area.

9. Now the newlywedded shaft and blade are ready to assume the personality of one of Victoriaville's different models. First a template is used to describe the specified shape and size of each blade blank. In the case of the pros, it is custom-designed to the player's own specifications.

10, 11. Next the blade is cut and sanded to a fine finish.

12. If a blade is to be curved, it is now put in special vises for final shaping. Again, in the case of the pros, these vises are shaped to each player's personal specifications.

13, 14. To prevent the blade from shattering, splintering, or breaking, fiberglass strips are impregnated into it under thousands of pounds of pressure, actually meshing with the wood and extending over the throat for added strength.

15, 16. Next, the blade and throat are lacquer-finished and the handle is decorated with stripes in the team's colors.

17. Before leaving the mill, each stick is stamped with the famous "Victoriaville Pro" trademark—a symbol of the quality, hand craftsmanship that has gone into it—and tested under pressure to assure that it will withstand the rigors of professional play.

18. Finally, carefully bundled to protect them during shipment, Victoriaville sticks are on their way to hockey players around the world—perhaps one day to be lifted ceilingward in triumph over a hat trick.

PEE-WEE AND HIS PALS *by Bill Reid*

Hockey Night in Southeast Asia

When the Japanese National Hockey Team came to Canada last February to play a 6-game exhibition schedule, there were a few surprises for the Canadian fans. Japanese hockey has improved tremendously in the past few years, largely as a result of a handful of Canadians who have worked with the Japanese since the inception of the Japanese Ice Hockey League in 1966.

Playing for the Japanese team was Toshimitsu Ohtsubo, a goalie who might be good enough to play in the NHL; Takao Hikigi, who reminds fans of the style of Jean Beliveau (although he's only 5'9" and 161 lbs.); and Tsutomu Hanzawa, who is a terrific back checker and skater, although he's only 5'3". Compared with a West German player at 6'9", and the two tallest players in the NHL, Bob Dailey (6'5½") of Vancouver and Pete Mahovlich (6'5") of Montreal, Hanzawa would look like a weed among the redwoods.

The success of this team is due in large part to the Canadians who have molded the Japanese into fine players. Also, a growing interest in winter sports in Japan has gone a long way to ensure the success of the National Team and the JIHL.

In Japan, the hockey season begins early in November, with the 60-game schedule being completed early in Febraury. Average attendance for the regular season games is about 4,000, with some games attracting as many as 10,000.

The Canadians primarily responsible for the development of Japanese hockey are Hitoshi (Herb) Wakabayashi, a league all-star and former U.S. college star from Chatham, Ontario; Terry O'Malley, former captain of Canada's National Team; Mel Wakabayashi, Herb's brother; and Dave Dies, a 31-year old Montrealer and former player and coach with McGill University and Sir George Williams University.

In the final game of the 1974 Season, the Ooji Seishi team captured the championship with an 8-5 victory. A player named Takao Hitsugi collected the hat trick while the Honma brothers, Japan's answer to the Hull and Mahovlich pair, each collected two goals. Herb Wakabayashi scored one of the five goals for the losers.

Wakabayashi, who would hardly stand out or rate much attention were he to play pro hockey in Canada, is a genuine superstar in Japan. It points out how far the Japanese still have to go to reach world class hockey standards.

But Herb tries to bring the standards up. Hockey in Japan has been a successful experience for Herb. He and his family have been treated well and supported well by the parent club, Seibu. He chose to take out Japanese citizenship, partly to feel more a part of the country, and partly to play for Japan's National Team in the Sapporo Olympics.

"When I was a foreign player here," Herb states, "everything went quite well, but since the change (in citizenship) it hasn't been quite as good."

But things haven't been all that bad. During the 1974 International Games, the Japanese National Team placed fourth in the "B" group. Impressive won-lost records have been logged by the two teams from which most of the all-star players on the National Team had been taken. Kokudo, 1974 champions in league regular season play, had a record of 16-2-2. The second place Seibu team finished the season at 15-3-2. It is from these teams that the majority of the National Team members were recruited to play an exhibition schedule in Canada.

While not up to the level of Canadian professional hockey, the interest is there, and the enthusiasm. Now, if the Japanese player, with his native genius for duplication and imitation, would follow the pattern of a Bobby Clarke or a Bobby Orr, Japanese hockey would reach big league standards in no time.

But if they all adopt the Eddie Shack style of play — or that of Dave Schultz — there would be pandemonium on the tiny island.

While the Japanese have only a few Canadian nationals to worry about, the hockey scene in Peking has an entire team of Canadians, and another team of Russians to cause the host country a host of migraines. This "Hockey Night" is complete with spies and intrigue ... and a lot of fun, even though the Canadians usually come out on the losing end. Yet, it sounds like everyone has a good time.

The story of the Canada/Russia hockey series, Peking style, was revealed in *The Globe and Mail*, on February 6, 1975. In this article, the name of Karl Duchesne, goalie for the Canadian side, was touted from coast to coast. He's the class of the Canadian-Peking side, without whom the score against the Canadians of over-the-hill hockey playing journalists and diplomats would be similar to to those of the Washington Capitals on an off night.

But this series has everything. It has Vladimir Korolov, the Russian forward and top goal scorer, who started the poor man's replay of the 1972 Series. Ambassadors, wives and children from all over the world. A Russian referee. A Russian goalie who wears workboots in the net. And a Dave Schultz-type, 225-pound, 6-foot Canadian "enforcer." The Peking series became the Russians against the Rest of the World, as the Canadians added other Nationals to their side.

The players have fun, and the diplomats keep both eyes and ears open for any state secrets that might be discussed while their teams are in action on the ice. Some even believe that agents of the KGB are there, just in case.

Played on an outdoor rink, the games in the series last only as long as the ice does, which is usually from Christmas until mid-February. Doubtless the Russians gloat over their many victories at the diplomatic lunches and teas. Doubtless the Canadians say "Wait until next year", when Air Canada might fly in a fresh load of reserves. In any case, no one in Peking is suggesting that either team contend for the Stanley Cup.

***
EVEN FOR
SUPERSTARS
THE ROAD TO THE
BIG LEAGUES
CAN BE BUMPY
***

Look at them out there on the ice! They do it all so well. Skating, shooting, stickhandling. They're the superstars. Names like Howe, Hull, Esposito, Orr and Park. They made it to the "bigs" (the big leagues) with ease. No sweat. Because they had the talent, man. The *talent*! When you've got the talent it's never any sweat. Or is it?

Did these guys ever have to work for what they've got? Did they ever know the pain of being cut from a tryout camp? Did they ever fight back tears when the coach said, "Son, we can't use you. Try again next year."

Well, did they?

When **Phil Esposito** was 13 years old he tried out for a bantam hockey team in Sault Ste. Marie. A lot of other guys tried out too. It was a good team called the Algoma Contractors coached by a man named Angelo Bombacco. Phil desperately wanted to make the team. He skated miles getting ready. He worked on his shot and his stickhandling. Phil was proud of his stickhandling and he *knew* he could handle the puck better than most of the other kids. He was big, too, and he thought that might give him an edge during the tryouts.

On the day of the tryout, he showed up on time. His skates were sharp and he carried a good stick. He got his chance and a fair amount of ice time but he really didn't get much opportunity to show off his stickhandling ability. And he must have looked a bit awkward . . . all elbows and knees. Because when the tryout was finished, coach Bombacco called off the names of 20 players and motioned them to one side. The others were told they could go home. They were the castoffs . . . the unwanted . . . the not-good-enoughs. Phil Esposito was among them. And he had tried so *hard*. In the dressing room, he broke down and cried.

A few weeks later, playing for another bantam team, Phil found himself up against the Algoma Contractors. He had the incentive . . . the desire . . . to do well . . . to show Angelo Bombacco that the big kid with the awkward style could play hockey. He scored several goals and Phil's team beat the Contractors soundly.

The next season Phil made the Contractors easily and Bombacco became his coach and friend for life.

But Phil often thinks of that day when he failed to make the team. How crushed he was and how the tears flowed.

Bobby Orr always had ability. His father, Doug Orr, spotted it right from the beginning. Doug Orr was an outstanding hockey prospect himself and might have played pro hockey had it not been for World War Two

when service in the Navy occupied most of his time. When Bobby played shinny with the other kids on the frozen Sequin River, near Parry Sound, Doug Orr was amazed at how easily he controlled the puck. The other kids would seldom steal it away from him. Trouble was ... Bobby was such a *little* guy. At age 12, he stood about five feet two and weighed about as much as a pair of goal pads.

His coach in those days was a former NHL star ... Bucko McDonald. Despite his small stature, Bucko placed Bobby on defense in pee wee hockey. The other players towered over him. The height and weight difference was even more obvious when Orr was invited to play with Bucko's Bantam All Stars in the All-Ontario playdowns.

When Doug Orr took the coach aside and suggested Bobby might feel more at home on a forward line, Bucko merely shook his head and said, "No ... your kid was born to play defense."

The Bantam All Stars from Parry Sound travelled to Gananoque, Ontario for an important playoff game. Several big league scouts were at the game, including five members of the Boston Bruins — team President Weston Adams, Sr., General Manager Lynn Patrick, Coach Milt Schmidt, and scouts "Baldy" Cotton and Wren Blair.

They were anxious to see two 14-year old prospects — both of whom played for Gananoque.

Blair will never forget that game. "I saw this little blond kid skate for Parry Sound and I chuckled because his pants were hanging down below his knees. His hockey jersey was too big for him and the elbows dropped down to his hockey gloves. What a sight! Then the game began and the kid took over. He amazed us all with the way he took charge of that game ... cradling passes like a pro, putting the puck on the sticks of his mates with incredible accuracy, always in position. When we talked about the game afterwards, all the other Bruin officials agreed they'd never seen anything like it. One of them said he could have played with the Bruins right then ... and looked right at home. And the kid was only 12 years old."

By the time he was 14, Bobby Orr was commuting twice a week to Oshawa, Ontario (a six hour drive round trip) to play junior A hockey with the Oshawa Generals. By the time he was 18 he was a rookie-of-the-year in the NHL with Boston.

Bobby never had to worry about not making a team. He was always a star. But he lost a lot of sleep wondering if he'd ever grow big enough to stop the big bruisers who play in the NHL.

As a youngster, growing up in Point Anne, Ontario, **Bobby Hull** developed a hockey flaw. He hogged the puck. It was a habit he didn't completely lose for many years.

It's easy to understand how Bobby became a puck hog. His first memories of hockey involve getting up on cold winter mornings, stoking the fires in the house, making himself a hot bowl of oatmeal, then dashing off to the Bay of Quinte or a local rink for an hour-long skate, or better still, a game of shinny before school.

Often, the skating sessions were preceded by some strenuous shovelling. Once the ice was clear of snow, dozens of kids scrambled after the puck in a shinny free-for-all. The biggest, strongest, fastest . . . controlled the puck. Passing the puck was not a popular pastime because a player never knew when he might get it back again. As a result, players hung onto the puck until an opposing player batted it away or a goal was scored. That's the style of hockey Bobby Hull played.

There came a day when Bobby Hull journeyed down the highway to Belleville. He was registered to play bantam hockey. The rink was jammed with kids when he showed up. They were all waiting for their team assignments. The P.A. announcer called off the names. Players moved to one corner of the rink or another. Finally, all the names had been called and Bobby stood there, alone. He had not been assigned a team. He was crushed, hurt and disappointed.

He skated over to a corner of the rink and hung back on the group assigned to one of the teams. He was desperate enough to plead with the coach there to add his name to the roster. He wanted desperately to belong.

Then, a voice called to him from another area of the rink. It was Dan Cowley, one of the coaches, a brother of Bill Cowley, who had been a famous star with the Boston Bruins.

"Come over here, Bobby! You're going to be on my team."

It was true. The P.A. announcer had skipped over Bobby's name by mistake. Disappointment turned to delight. Bobby had found a team.

Other teams followed and Bobby's goal-scoring exploits attracted the attention of Chicago Black Hawk scouts. By age 16, he was playing for the Jr. A St. Catherines Black Hawks.

As a center, he took dead aim at the goal line and made many spectacular solo rushes. His coach, Rudy Pilous, wanted him to pass more often and so did the fans. The criticism bothered him and he scored only eleven goals in his first year of junior hockey.

In his second season, Pilous took him aside and told him he was going to move him to left wing. "Maybe then you'll pass more often," Bobby was told. Bobby argued the point with his coach and was suspended. He packed up and went home to Point Anne. His parents talked to him about the situation and advised him how to deal with it.

Bobby returned to St. Catherines and apologized to Pilous. But he didn't change his style of play. And the next season, any further friction was averted when Bobby made it all the way to the NHL.

Looking back, he feels he shouldn't have been allowed to play such an individual role in minor hockey. His first coaches should have insisted he pass more often and not hog the puck. Criticism of his one-man gang efforts took some of the enjoyment out of his minor hockey play. It wasn't until he turned professional and became more "hockey-wise" did he realize how important teamwork was to success.

When **Brad Park** was just a kid, his dad worked part time as a referee. Brad was too young to play organized hockey but he enjoyed going to the games and watching his dad work.

One day a goaltender failed to show up for a game and Brad leaped at the chance to play. "I'm a goalie," he lied. "Give me some goal pads and I'll play for you guys."

Brad didn't know a thing about goaltending but he wanted to play hockey so badly he'd play anywhere. They helped him dress for the game and they pushed him out on the ice. He shuffled into the net and turned around just in time to see a rival forward hurtling toward him. Brad braced himself, hoping the player would shoot for the short side. But the shot came sliding in and sailed into the far corner of the net. One shot . . . one goal!

Brad Park turned his back to the play and cried. Here he had a chance to play in a real hockey game and he muffed the first shot to come his way.

He wiped his tears away and made up his mind to do better. He jumped around the net and made some awkward saves. He played another game . . . then a third . . . and whenever a player moved in on him he sprawled across the crease because he noticed few of his opponents could lift the puck. He was soon accepted and when the coach discovered he could skate well, he was moved to a forward position and in no time at all he was the scoring star of the team.

By age 12, he was a member of the Scarboro team that breezed to victory in the championship game at the prestigious International Pee Wee Tournament in Quebec City. One of his teammates was Syl Apps, Jr. who, like Brad went to stardom in the NHL.

Growing up in St. Catherines, Ontario, after emigrating from Czechoslovakia to live with his uncle Joe and aunt Anna, **Stan Mikita** became a bona fide "rink rat." A rink rat is a hockey-mad youngster who spends every spare minute possible in the rink.

In Stan's case, Vic Teal, his bantam hockey coach, was chief engineer at the St. Catharines' arena. "Stan showed me something," Vic recalled one time. "He had it inside himself to excel . . . to be the best around."

So Teal helped young Mikita. Teal had played a lot of minor league hockey and he knew all the tricks. He recognized Mikita's sloppy playing habits and taught him proper techniques. Under Teal's tutelage, Mikita learned how to check properly. He introduced drills that helped to improve Stan's skating, stickhandling and shooting. More important, he allowed Stan to use the ice in the arena. Stan became one of

several rink rats who showed up at dawn. In return for practice time, Stan and his pals did odd jobs around the rink. They swept under the seats, scraped the ice and put out the garbage.

Teal was a disciplinarian. He would not tolerate players who broke rules or talked back. He particularly disliked players who smoked.

Teal had a habit of whacking errant players on the backside with a broom when they misbehaved or failed to perform a hockey drill to the satisfaction of the coach.

One day a hulking defenseman snapped back at the coach after feeling the broom thud into his backside. He swore at Teal and Mikita, standing nearby, added his two cents worth.

Teal ordered them both out of the arena and told them never to come back.

For a day or two the players were content to keep busy with other activities. Then it dawned on Stan that there was a void in his life. Suddenly, there was no more hockey. It hurt.

He went back to Vic Teal and apologized. Teal refused to believe that Stan really meant it. Then Stan began to cry and Teal was convinced. He gave Stan a second chance.

"I'll let you back in the rink," he said. "But no more smoking or talking back."

If it hadn't been for Vic Teal, Stan Mikita might never have made it to the NHL.

Surely **Gordie Howe**, the greatest player of them all, was a hockey prodigy, a brilliant teenager who attracted national headlines at an early age.

No, it wasn't that way at all. Oh, Gordie was a good hockey player, all right. No question about that.

At age 15, he was invited to attend a New York Ranger tryout camp in Winnipeg. He went but he was homesick and he felt awkward and ill at ease with the older players. In fact, he knew so little about the modern equipment he was issued, he had to watch the other boys to figure out what went where.

112

Especially the athletic supporter. He'd never owned one.

After a few days, homesickness got the better of him and he beat a hasty retreat back home to Saskatoon.

The next offer came from the Detroit Red Wings. Would Gordie travel all the way to Windsor, Ontario to attend a try-out camp? He would . . . only if some of the guys he knew in Saskatoon would be going along too. As it turned out, several Saskatoon players were Detroit-bound and Gordie actually looked forward to this excursion. Gordie showed enough in Windsor for the Red Wings to want to keep him in Eastern Canada. He was sent to Galt, Ontario to play junior hockey. But there was a snag. He needed a release from his league in Western Canada and for one full season he merely practiced with the Galt team and was not allowed to play. It was called "establishing residence."

Detroit's plan to have Gordie play in Galt the following season never materialized. It was decided to turn him professional with Omaha, a Red Wing farm club. He signed for $2700 for the season and was ecstatic with the contract. He even went out and celebrated by buying a single beer. And he put every spare penny away. That season he saved $1700.

"I figured I'd better save my money," he recalls. "I didn't know for sure how long anybody would want to pay me good money for playing hockey. In fact, I remember my biggest ambition was to just hang on as a member of the Red Wings for a full season. Then I could go back home and brag about it to all the folks back home."

Think about how many times the hockey scouts have been wrong when they appraised the good little guys in hockey. Oh, you won't get many of them to admit it now. They'll say, "It must have been some other scout. I always knew the kid would make it."

But it's true there were many hockey experts who looked at **Marcel Dionne** when he started out in junior hockey. "Too small," they said sadly. "Too small to stand the grind of the big league schedule. Too small to take any guff in the corners. Those big defensemen will simply pick the kid up and stuff him in their pocket . . . or slide him through a

crack in the boards and that'll be the end of that."

Even when Marcel Dionne was drafted number 1 by Detroit during the summer draft meetings in 1971, it was a well-known fact that the Red Wings agonized over the selection. Would they have been better off to have taken hulking defenseman Jocelyn Guevremont or sharp-shooting Richard Martin?

Everybody, it seems, was concerned about Dionne's size (or lack of it) ... everybody but Dionne.

He simply went out and chalked up 77 points in his rookie season, an all-time record in the NHL.

He followed up with seasons of 90 points in 1972-3 and 78 points in 1973-4. Last season he finished fourth in the NHL scoring race with 121 points.

Now the hockey men don't mention his size anymore. In fact, they haven't said much about Dionne's small stature in quite some time.

Perhaps they've been too busy studying the moves of pint-sized prodigies, players like Bobby Lalonde, Danny Gare and Doug Palazzarri of St. Louis and muttering among themselves, "Too small, too small ... what a shame ... they're all too small."

One Los Angeles King who has been a standout is captain **Terry Harper**, a player who is all heart and hard work. These credentials helped him make it to the NHL and they have kept him there for 13 seasons.

Terry's desire to excel was first evident after a serious accident almost took his life when he was twelve years old. He was pouring gasoline on some smoldering trash outside his Regina home when the can exploded. Terry was rushed to hospital where he spent the next six months undergoing skin grafts to most of his body. It was touch and go whether Terry would ever be able to function properly again ... if he survived.

Survive he did, and function he learned to do ... all over again. Before long he was back on the ice, determined to ignore his scars and become a hockey player.

This desire attracted the attention of the Montreal Canadiens, and Harper's hard work earned him a spot on the Montreal roster in 1962.

Traded to Los Angeles in 1972, Terry is the acknowledged team leader and one of the most respected players in the game today.

His desire to excel has carried over into other pursuits. Terry has his private pilot's license, he designs hockey equipment and he's an excellent fisherman and scuba diver.

Eddie Shack and some of the Leafs attended the athletic awards ceremonies at a prison near Toronto. Shack drew the biggest laugh of the night when he told the inmates: "The only difference between me and you guys is you guys GOT CAUGHT!"

Stemkowski (again) "Am I glad my mother named me Peter."
Bystander: "Why?"
Stemmer: "Cause that's what everybody calls me."

Bob Haggert, former Leaf trainer, tells this Ron Stewart story. Stewart was hurt one night and the club doctor informed him, in the Gardens hospital, that his arm was broken and he'd be sidelined a couple of months. "Tell me, doc," Stewart said "will I be able to play the piano when it's healed?" "I don't see why not," was the reply. "That's strange," Stewart said. "I couldn't play the piano before."

SON OF SUPERFAN

Terence V. Kelly, Q.C., is a lawyer from Oshawa, Ontario. Terence V. Kelly is also a sports fanatic. He's a sports fan like no other sports fan. In fact, he's such a fan he's been described in SPORTS ILLUSTRATED as Superfan. A criminal lawyer, Superfan has been known to win a quick acquittal for a client, dash for the nearest airport and be seated at a ball game, a soccer match, a Stanley Cup playoff game hundreds of miles away, often before the trial judge has had time to dismiss the jury and doff his robes for the day.

Terence V. Kelly never concerns himself about getting tickets for important sports events. He simply arrives on the scene of the chosen event and inevitably comes up with choice seats. How does he do it? "Well, I've got a bit of Irish luck, I guess," says Kelly. "Plus a bit of gall and confidence. Even if a sports contest is sold out weeks in advance I have faith that I'll be able to get in somehow . . . even if I show at the last moment. It doesn't seem to matter if it's the Grey Cup, the Stanley Cup or the World Cup. I always manage to get in, and usually with good seats too."

Tim Kelly is the son of Terence V. Kelly. He's the son of Superfan. How lucky can a guy be? Imagine this. You're sitting at home doing your homework. Dad rushes in, begins throwing things in a travel bag and hollers at you, "Tim, grab some clean clothes and bring your toothbrush. Let's try to catch the deciding game in the Stanley Cup finals." And off you go.

Son of Superfan has been on some memorable junkets.

Recently, I asked him to send along his impressions of one of them. Here's what he wrote:

B.M.

My name is Tim Kelly and like most 14-year olds I'm a sports fanatic.

However, I'd say I'm one of the few lucky ones who's been able to see his favorite sports figures in action around the globe.

I've been on many trips, most of them in North America, but my best trip was undoubtedly my World Cup of Soccer extravaganza of 1974. This competition, held in West Germany, took three weeks from mid-June to the first week of July. During this time we saw 13 of 38 games in 9 cities, including the World Cup Final in Munich. However, since this book is about hockey, I'd like to give you "My best hockey trip."

This trip was taken in March of 1972 and included stops in Buffalo, Washington, Philadelphia, Boston, New York,

Tim with Jacques Plante at a 1974 Maple Leaf practice.

Toronto, Detroit, Milwaukee Minneapolis, St. Louis, Chicago and finally Toronto again.

We (my father and I) started on March 17 on a short flight to Buffalo. Immediately following the flight we headed to Buffalo's Memorial Auditorium to see the Sabres and the Vancouver Canucks. The Sabres suffered a 6-2 defeat and it was hard to believe then, that these two teams, who were 7 - 8 in Eastern Division that year, would be 1st place powers in 1974-75. They had little to offer this night.

The next morning we took an early flight to Washington, D.C. This section of the trip was mainly educational. I still can't believe how much we did on this day. We got a taxi to give us a tour of Washington. We visited the Washington Monument, the Lincoln Memorial, the Capitol, the White House, the Kennedy Grave-sites at Arlington, the Supreme Court House and the Smithsonian Institution, all by about 4 o'clock. I love

history and this part of the trip was very enthralling.

At about 4 p.m. we took a short flight to Philadelphia for an eight o'clock game at the Spectrum. The strong New York Rangers beat a hapless Flyer team 5 - 3. To everyone's disappointment an injured Bobby Clarke played a measly 3 minutes.

The next morning we flew to Boston for an afternoon encounter between the Bruins and the Minnesota North Stars. This was a nationally televised game and some of you may remember that vicious stick-swinging incident between Wayne Cashman and Dennis Hextall. It resulted in a 3-game suspension for the two participants. Anyway, a strong Bruin unit crunched a weak North Star team 7 - 3.

With ten minutes to go, we left the Garden and took a short flight to New York. That night we saw a play-off bound Leaf team dumped 5 - 3 by the Rangers at Madison Square Garden. Ed

With Gump Worsley outside Boston Gardens, March 19, 1972.

Giacomin was the highlight of the game, with two assists. This was our fourth game in three days!

From here we flew back to Toronto, to pick up my only sister, Jane, who was eight years old.

We then flew on to Minneapolis with stops in Detroit and Milwaukee. We spent two days in Minneapolis at Wren Blair's house. Mr. Blair had known my father for some time and they were good friends, thus the room and board.

On Tuesday, April 21st, we saw the North Stars play the California Golden

After the game between Philadelphia Eagles and Buffalo Bills, Rich Stadium, Orchard Park, N.Y., 1973.

Seals. The Seals lost 4 - 2. There was a larger treat ahead, however.

The Seals' manager, Garry Young, who once worked in our home-town, Oshawa, Ontario, asked my dad if we wanted to fly with the Seals on to St. Louis. Dad heartily agreed.

We took a very late flight and Reggie Leach took a liking to Jane. The two of

With Tom Seaver, Wrigley Field, 1973.

With Jane at Comiskey Park, Chicago, 1972.

117

With Alex Delvecchio in Chicago after Detroit beat the Black Hawks 2-0.

Superfan

them must have eye-winked each other till they could barely see.

On Wednesday night we saw the Seals beaten 4 - 1 by the stronger Blues.

We then flew on to Chicago, a move I still don't understand. We didn't see any sporting events there, seeing only the Cub and White Sox parks only a few weeks before the opening of the 1972 season.

On Thursday night we flew back to Toronto, ending our trip. We'd seen six games in six days. We'd seen great historic sites, great personalities (Gump Worsley in Boston, Wren Blair and the Seals team) and of course we'd had a great time.

I've been on other trips, usually during the summer to see baseball, and during the winter, basketball, hockey or football, or a combination, each year. Of course there's the odd special trip like the World Cup trip.

I've been overseas twice; once in 1971 when I saw some English Soccer matches, and of course, the 1974 trip which included a 3-day stop in England to see Jimmy Connors at Wimbledon.

I've mainly visited the United States Eastern Coastal area and the Midwest, but I've never visited the West Coast. I plan to soon. I also plan to tour Europe and also to visit Argentina in 1978 for the next World Cup of Soccer.

As far as favorite sports goes, I enjoy soccer the most, followed together by

Son of Superfan with Pele, Munich, 1974.

baseball, football, basketball and hockey. Incidentally we share season's tickets for the Toronto Maple Leafs, hold four season's tickets for the O.H.A. Junior "A" Oshawa Generals and also have season's tickets for the exciting Buffalo Bills.

I would have to say I've been very lucky, and to you young sports fanatics out there, there is nothing like traveling the globe to see your favorite sports heroes live and in action.

In 1903 a game between Ottawa and Rat Portage was held up for 15 minutes while a search was made for a puck to replace the one being used. It fell through a hole in the ice

In 1904 the first line was used when it was decided to paint a black line across the goalmouth. The game was between The Winnipeg Rowing Club and Ottawa.

When the Pacific Coast Hockey Association was introduced in 1911 the players also acted as referees and goal judges.

In 1909 Edmonton challenged Montreal Wanderers for the Stanley Cup. Edmonton did not have one player who played a game for them in 1909. They "imported" such stars as Bert Lindsay, Didier Pitre, Lester Patrick and many others. Montreal won handily.

In 1911 Montreal Canadiens were allowed to sign French-speaking players only.

In late 1913 Sprague Cleghorn was fined heavily in a Toronto court of law for "having struck an opponent with a hockey stick." There was talk he would be barred for life from the game but he ignored a lengthy "suspension" and played after missing a single game.

ROGIE VACHON

KING OF KINGS

"He's the smallest goalie in the NHL. He's the quickest, the smartest, the coolest ... the best."

This can only describe one man ... Rogie Vachon, chief puckstopper with the L.A. Kings.

In Philadelphia they mutter similar remarks about Bernie Parent, deleting the word "smallest," of course, and in Montreal, they change "smallest" to "biggest" and apply much the same sort of praise to Ken Dryden.

No matter. In Los Angeles, Rogatien Rosaire Vachon reigns as King of the goaltenders. King of the Kings. Even fans of the Parents, the Drydens and the Tony Espositos of the hockey world find it difficult to argue against Rogie's royal title. And during the 1974-75 season readers of the *Hockey News* named Rogie Player-of-the-Year in the NHL, so he must be at the peak of his profession.

It's true he's quick, smart, cool ... and completely unflappable. When he gets upset over a missed goal, it's only with himself. He feels he should stop every shot ... which is impossible, of course. Seconds later, that particular shot is forgotten and he's back to concentrating on stopping the next one.

With Rogie in goal, the Kings surged to a team record 105 points in 1974-75. Without him, they never would have stayed so close to Montreal, winners of the Norris Division.

It's a long way from Rogie's home town of Palmarolle, Quebec, to Los Angeles. But he enjoys the California life style. Carrying golf clubs or a beach towel is more fun than hoisting a snow shovel, somehow.

Rogie's life is full. He has a beautiful wife (Nicole), a son Nicholas, an adopted South Vietnamese war orphan named Jade and a fancy sports car worth $15,000.

He's the key player on a team that appears to be getting stronger every year.

Rogie can think of only one thing that would make him completely happy.

The Stanley Cup.

HOCKEY NICKNAMES

Below you will find a list of 40 hockey players, past and present, who are commonly referred to by their nicknames. The first 20 are easy; for those of you who solve them, the other 20 are more challenging. Match the names in the left-hand column with the nicknames on the right. The answers can be found at the back of the book.

1. Yvon Cournoyer	1. Rocket
2. Bernie Geoffrion	2. The Cat
3. Emile Francis	3. Howie
4. George Armstrong	4. Turk
5. Pat Stapleton	5. The Hammer
6. Brian Spencer	6. Cowboy
7. Derek Sanderson	7. Boom Boom
8. Hector Blake	8. Punch
9. Maurice Richard	9. The Road Runner
10. Frank Mahovlich	10. Swoop
11. George Imlach	11. Pit
12. Jim McKenny	12. The Eel
13. Miles Horton	13. Spinner
14. Dave Schultz	14. Gump
15. Lorne Worsley	15. The Chief
16. Bill Flett	16. Moose
17. Hubert Martin	17. Toe
18. Camille Henry	18. Tim
19. Andre Dupont	19. Whitey
20. Wayne Carleton	20. The Big M
21. Elmer Lach	21. Baldy
22. Gerry Toppazini	22. Butch
23. Harold Cotton	23. Teeder
24. Edouard Lalonde	24. The Big Train
25. Emile Bouchard	25. Le Gros Bill
26. Francis Clancy	26. Muzz
27. Jean Beliveau	27. Busher
28. Ted Kennedy	28. Spider
29. Gordie Howe	29. Dit
30. Eddie Mazur	30. Hap
31. Lionel Conacher	31. Topper
32. Mike Walton	32. Pie
33. Murray Patrick	33. Leapin' Lou
34. Leighton Emms	34. Newsy
35. Floyd Curry	35. Blinky
36. Aubrey Clapper	36. Turk
37. Ted Lindsay	37. King
38. John MacKenzie	38. Scarface
39. Walter Broda	39. The Old Lamplighter
40. Louis Fontinato	40. Shaky

HE CARES ABOUT HOCKEY'S HISTORY

It's a good thing that Bill Galloway is a hockey nut. Otherwise, the history of hockey in North America might be missing some key elements.

Like a photographic record of the game's progress, for example. And motion picture film of the hockey's big moments, from early day play to the most recent Stanley Cup finals.

Since 1969, Bill Galloway has supervised a program for the development of a National Film Collection in Canada.

In half a dozen years he has collected over 16,000,000 feet of film relating to Canada, much of it footage relating to the nation's sporting past.

Possibly because Galloway is wild about hockey, his film collection of the ice sport's development ranks as the best in the world.

How big is best?

"I estimate I have acquired well over 1.5 million feet of film relating to hockey," he states. "And I'm adding to

"This early-day hockey game is between a couple of college teams in Montreal. Two posts stuck in the ice served as goals. Note the low boards, high snowbanks.

123

The year is 1910. Hockey men in Renfrew, Ontario, spent thousands of dollars importing top stars in an unsuccessful attempt to "buy" the Stanley Cup. Fred (Cyclone) Taylor, Lester Patrick and Bert Lindsay (Ted's dad) were members of the Renfrew team.

the collection all the time. For example, I was interviewed on Hockey Night in Canada a year ago and made a quiet plea for leads to additional film. The response was overwhelming. I received mail from dozens of people who knew of some vintage film or photographs tucked away in attic trunks and basement closets.

"Later on, I was interviewed again, this time on the NBC hockey telecasts and again there was a welcome mail response from American viewers. I never realized how much film footage was in the hands of private citizens, collectors, newsreel agencies and other groups.

"Gradually, I'm compiling a vivid record of hockey events and personalities that go all the way back to before the turn of the century."

Galloway believes he has obtained for the Public Archives the first-ever images of hockey on film, taken about 1898.

"It appears the cameraman, using a primitive motion picture camera, asked two teams of off-duty railroad workers

Early-day goal judges wore heavy clothing (in this case a raccoon coat) and stood right out on the ice behind the net. If a goal was scored, they waved a white handkerchief.

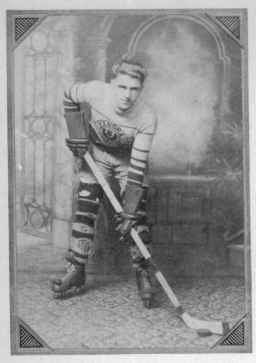

An unidentified early-day star with the Kenora Thistles poses in the photographer's studio. Note the felt padding over the toes of the skates, the tattered hockey pants, the "holy" stockings.

to line up in front of his camera and bat a puck back and forth. They did but the game that resulted wasn't very exciting. The players, obviously intrigued with the novelty of the situation, spent more time mugging at the camera and trying to upstage each other than they did whacking at the puck."

His collection of hockey photographs, or stills, is matching the growth rate of the film collection.

"People have been generous," says Galloway. "I make it clear that what they turn over to me does not become my personal property. They can either donate it to the Canadian people outright or they can have it filed as their personal collection. Eventually, it's stored in the Public Archives in Ottawa."

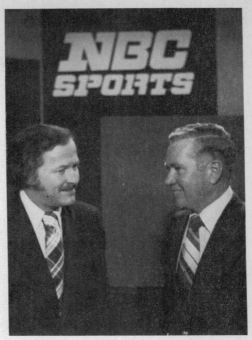

Bill Galloway and the author.

Over the past few years, Galloway has discovered a film record of such hockey events as the opening night ceremonies at Maple Leaf Gardens, Gordie Howe's first few NHL goals (he scored just seven in his rookie season), the famous St. Patrick's Day riot at the Montreal Forum, and Bobby Hull's record-breaking performances in the sixties. He even has an early-day Stanley Cup parade through the muddy streets of Ottawa.

While hockey footage occupies a prominent place in the Public Archives' vaults, other sports are also well-represented.

"I may get a tip on some hockey footage," says Galloway, "and wind up with film of a memorable prizefight or football game. Recently, a collector donated a complete boxing match featuring Tommy Burns, the only Canadian to win the world heavyweight boxing title."

A 46-year old bachelor, Galloway travels thousands of miles every year in his search for film and photos. A star

125

For many years, the players "centering" squared off in the manner filmed above. Their backs were toward the side boards, not the end boards. Note the fancy uniform on the referee.

Early-day goaltenders often wore caps or hats, not only to keep their heads warm but to protect themselves from young lads with peashooters in the crowd. Note the elbow pad outside the jersey and the primitive gloves. This goalie's name was Charles Teno.

You probably don't remember the New York Americans. The team was composed mainly of players from the Hamilton Tigers. The Tigers went on strike for more playoff money in 1924, and the next season the Hamilton franchise was transferred to New York. This was the first training camp for the Americans. The referee is T.P. Gorman. Red Green is facing off with Eddie Bouchard. The near defenseman in the foreground (wearing a striped Hamilton jersey) is Ken Randall, hockey's "bad boy" of that era.

At least once a team wore jerseys with football numerals. In this wild brawl between the Rangers and the Canadiens in March, 1925, number 64 is Armand Mondou. He took the first penalty shot in the NHL . . . and missed.

The Stanley Cup parade, 1923. This photo, taken right from the film of the event, shows the lead car. T.P. Gorman was manager of the team and King Clancy was a young defenseman.

hockey player in his youth, Galloway now confines his active participation in sport to golf, where he seeks par as eagerly as he seeks old film.

"Old film," he says, "deteriorates quickly. Particularly old nitrate stock. But much of it can be restored by means of modern technical advances and it should be transferred to new safety film.

What's more, nitrate stock is highly flammable so there's always the danger of losing an important slice of Canadian history."

Any old film in your basement? Photographs? Records? Historical documents? Drop the man a note.

Write Bill Galloway, Public Archives of Canada, Ottawa K1A 0N3, Ontario.

PEE-WEE AND HIS PALS by Bill Reid

HOCKEY QUIZ

This quiz will tell you how much (or how little) you know about the duties of the minor officials in the NHL. Be careful . . . it's a tough one. If you get four out of five correct answers, you really know your hockey. Five out of five and you are an expert.

Select the answer which is most nearly correct.

A. A player is sent to the penalty box. During his penalty he turns to the penalty time keeper and asks, "How much time is left in my penalty?"

   The time keeper replies:
1. "Under the NHL rules, I am not permitted to tell you."
2. "Look up the scoreboard clock and you'll see for yourself."
3. "You have (gives time remaining) left in your penalty."
4. "None of your business."

B. At the conclusion of each of the NHL games, the official scorer is required to distribute copies of the game score sheets in the following manner. He gives:

1. One copy to the Hockey News.
2. Three copies for distribution to the following parties:
   One each to:
   a. The League President.
   b. The visiting coach or manager.
   c. The home coach or manager.
3. Two copies to the home team owner and six copies to Clarence Campbell.
4. One copy to other NHL and WHA clubs.

C. The game timekeeper, to assist in assuring the prompt return to the ice of the teams for each period, shall:

1. Give a five minute warning by means of a buzzer.
2. Give a preliminary warning three minutes prior to the start of each period.
3. Pound on each team's dressing room door with his fist two minutes prior to the start of the period.
4. Ring a gong with a mallet.

D. NHL goal judges must abide by the following regulations:

1. They must be former players or referees.
2. They must sit in properly screened cages, stationed behind the goals and they must not change goals.
3. They must not wear glasses.
4. They must bring their own stools.

E. The game timekeeper shall provide:

1. Time of start and finish of each period.
2. Time taken for TV commercials.
3. Time both teams arrived for game.
4. Time of every whistle stopping play.

(Answers at the back of the book)

EMILE FRANCIS

They call Emile Francis the Cat. He's a cat with nine tales. All of them funny. Francis acquired the nickname Cat because of his nimble moves as a goaltender. In the past decades his moves as general manager and coach of the N.Y. Rangers are more notable than any he made while playing goal.

Still, his goaltending career deserves a quick review.

He came out of North Battleford, Saskatchewan, a 5'5" bundle of energy and jumped from amateur ranks right into the NHL.

Toward the close of the 1946-47 season he was called upon to replace Paul Bibeault in the Chicago goal. In those days the Black Hawk defense was paper-thin and the Cat's goals-against record was less than glittering.

"I remember the first time I came to play in Maple Leaf Gardens," the Cat recalls. "The Leafs bombed me for nine goals and one of the Toronto writers said that I'd never stay in the league because I was far too small. I was stopping forty and fifty shots a game."

"Anyway, the next time I ran into this guy, I told him 'It's not my height that's the trouble. It's just that if I'm going to sit in the wrong end of a shooting gallery, I'm going to have to grow a whole lot *wider*.'"

During his career, Emile played for 11 teams, including Chicago and New

York in the NHL. Minor league stops included Cleveland, New Haven and Cincinnati in the AHL, Vancouver, Seattle, Spokane, Saskatoon and Victoria in the Western League, and Kansas City in the old United States Hockey League.

Francis has always had a tendency to become involved in bitter arguments with goal judges. He was playing with

130

New Haven one night when Buffalo scored a disputed goal to tie the game. Francis blew his top when he saw the light go on. He tried to ram his goal stick through the wire mesh and into the face of goal judge, George Bach. Bach countered by calmly pulling out his hankerchief and blowing his nose. Francis then tried to leap over the screen to get at Bach but a spectator knocked him down and the brawl was on. There was such an uproar that the referee had the goal judge removed . . . for his own protection. Bach never came back.

Another time, in another place, a puck hit the goal post beside Francis and bounced into the corner of the rink. "I looked behind me," recalls Emile, "and the red light was on. I couldn't believe it. I rushed in there and demanded to know why the goal judge flashed the light when the puck obviously didn't go in. You know what he said? He said that was for the time he should have put the light on in the first period but failed to. And I thought I'd heard everything."

Francis had an interesting yarn to tell about a game played in Spokane.

"This was one time I got a break. I had a goal scored on me that didn't count. Jackie McLeod was with Saskatoon and he knocked the puck in behind me. But I grabbed it quick (like a Cat) and hauled it out of there before the goal judge could react. McLeod threw a fit when the goal was disallowed. He fumed and argued with the officials, and then, because we were good pals off the ice, he appealed to me. He said, 'Come on, Cat. Tell the referee it went in.' Well, friendship doesn't mean a thing in a close hockey game because I replied, 'Jackie, let's you and I just keep it a secret between ourselves.' McLeod got so mad he

wound up with a ten minute misconduct."

Even though he was a little fellow, Francis soon learned how to look after himself in pro hockey. When he first broke into the NHL a veteran forward wound up and drilled a shot at his head. Emile ducked and the puck sailed over the net. The forward growled in passing, "Better watch out, kid. I'm firin' them high tonight." The next time the player strayed near his net, the Cat took his goal stick and chopped the high shooter right across the ankles. As the player howled in pain, Francis warned, "Better watch out, pal. I'm hittin' low tonight."

A couple of seasons back, Emile hustled around behind the protective glass at Madison Square Gardens to argue a call with a goal judge. A fan got into it and soon the coats were off and the battle was on. The Ranger players came to their coach's aid. Three or four of them climbed the glass and leaped to the Cat's rescue. In doing so, one of them landed on Emile's suit coat, skates first, and sliced a few neat holes in it.

"I don't really get involved in too many disputes," claims Emile. "Oh, there was one time in Cleveland when Buddy Boone and I got involved in a stick-swinging duel. Then, on my way to the dressing room I was still sore so when a policeman got in my way I gave him a shove. After the game, four big cops came into the dressing room. They wanted to take me down to the station. My buddy, Freddie Glover, stood up, bless him, and said, 'If you want to take the Cat, you'll have to take 18 other players along with him.' That Glover always was a tough customer and the cops knew it. They left without another word."

During a game in U.S. college hockey, one of the players on our team was tripped and fell heavily into the boards. He was knocked unconscious and his teammates rushed to his aid.

One of them, Joe McLean, crouched down, and when the injured player's eyes blinked open, Joe enquired, "Eddie, if you die, may I have your skates?"

So You Want To Be A Goalie?

In the opinion of most hockey men, the goalie is the most important player on the ice. Hockey is a game of mistakes. If a forward or a defenseman makes a mistake, a teammate often covers up for him. When a goalie makes a mistake, it usually results in a goal.

Therefore, a goalie must be able to . . .

1. Accept responsibility and react well to pressure.
2. Play without fear.
3. Accept the fact that goals will be scored against him and not get discouraged.
4. Watch the puck and concentrate on the play at all times.
5. Move quickly on his skates from side to side.
6. Cut down the angles.
7. Decide quickly when to leave the net in a race for the puck. He who hesitates is often lost.
8. Move hands and feet and body quickly. This is often called having "quick reflexes."
9. Catch well with the gloved hand.
10. Get up and down quickly.

NHL goalies have mastered all the above rules and more, such as controlling rebounds and studying the moves of NHL forwards.

One of the stars—Dryden in action.

From: *The Chicago Tribune Magazine, January 19, 1975*

Hockey Mania

*Don't tell the Canadians just yet, but their national
pastime got out. Now 20,000 kids in the Chicago area
are sharpening skates and skills.*

BY JOHN BLADES

There was no reason for Judy Pigozzi
to be alarmed when her husband, Ray,
went to that first meeting 10 years ago.
Had she known what was ahead, however, she might have been tempted to
bolt the front door and risk a tripping
penalty if he tried to pass. It was a meeting of the Evanston Boys Hockey Association, and life in the Pigozzi household hasn't been quite the same since.
Not with four All-Star hockey players in
the family.

The Pigozzi sons — Ray Jr., 18, Tom,
17, Bob, 15, and Andy, 9 — have taken to
the ice as naturally and aggressively as
bear cubs to honey. So has their father.
In his youth, Ray Pigozzi was a stick boy
for Black Hawk opponents at Chicago
Stadium. Now he coaches an All-Star
Midget team (which includes son Bob)
and is an assistant coach for the Evanston High hockey team (which last year
included not only Bob but Ray Jr. and
Tom as well).

The feminine side of the Pigozzi family hasn't been immune to the mania
either. Daughter Ellen, 14, belongs to
the Evanston Speed Skating Club. And
Judy Pigozzi? Until her sons started
playing, she says only partly in jest, "All
I knew about hockey was that it was
played with a stick. I was dragged into
this kicking and screaming." She has
stopped kicking but not screaming.
Spirited and excitable, Mrs. Pigozzi
usually leads the cheering section when
one or more of her sons is on the ice.
"We can always hear her during the
games," kids Tom, "louder than anyone
else."

With so many players and fans under
one roof, the Pigozzis just may be the
first family of community hockey (on
north-suburban circuits, anyway). But if
the title does belong to them, it hasn't
been earned without a few headaches.
There's hardly an hour of the day when
at least one Pigozzi isn't off somewhere
on skates. Because ice rinks are as con-
gested as bowling alleys and tennis
courts, that has meant "horrendous
hours and distances" for the Pigozzis
(and hundreds of other hockey fam-
ilies), Judy says. In Andy's Squirt division, games are played as early as 6 a.m.
and as far away as Kenosha, so reveille is
at 4 a.m. when Ray or Judy has to do the
chauffeuring.

With Ray Jr. away at the University of
North Dakota, a little of the pressure's
off now, but Tom and Bob each play for
two teams, which means a double
schedule of games and practice. As a
result, a meal with all the Pigozzis at the
table is a rare event; dinner "hour", says
Judy, lasts from 5 to 10 p.m. "I have to
fix dishes that are easy to reheat — cas-
seroles, stews, spaghetti, things like
that."

Hockey has brought the Pigozzis

more than just headaches; the boys have also suffered their share of bruises, cuts, torn muscles, and sprains. They've been such regular visitors to the Evanston Hospital emergency room—both Ray Jr. and Bob ended up on examination tables after one rough game — that Mrs. Pigozzi says, "They should consider putting up a plaque in our honor." Ray Jr. has been the most seriously marked up; a head-on encounter with another player's skate left him with a gash on the brow that required 60 stitches, and he's the only one to lose a tooth (that was before mouth guards became standard league equipment). Compared with that, his brothers' wounds have all been of minor-league caliber.

What has been almost as painful, for the whole family, is the high price of playing hockey. "It's a rich man's game," says Ray Pigozzi, who is not a rich man. A stocky, taciturn architect (he designed the new Crown Center in Evanston) Pigozzi, 46, has always paid half of the $200 it costs his older boys just for a season's "ice time." The rest they have to earn themselves, either from part-time jobs or by selling $1 hockey-association stickers door to door (though with 600 boys in the Evanston program, that's not exactly a bull market.)

Besides the registration fees, there's a formidable investment in equipment — a team usually supplies its players only with jerseys. For starters, the Pigozzi brothers pay $125 for a pair of skates, which have to be sharpened every other game (for $1.50) and replaced every two years. They buy their $7 hockey sticks by the dozen. Then there are helmets, gloves, pants, shoulder, elbow, and shin pads, mouth guards, tape. . . . "I'd hate to add it all up," says Ray Pigozzi.

Another suburban parent did try adding it all up. Claire Ackermann of Niles sat down with an adding machine one day to see how much it cost her three sons to play for one year. "I nearly had a heart attack," she says. "When I figured

equipment, fees, travel, and camp, it came to $1,800."

No matter how traumatic the cost, it wasn't steep enough for Mrs. Ackermann to yank her sons from their teams. Nor did it cool her own enthusiasm for the sport. When I encountered her, Mrs. Ackermann was at a high-school game, strenuously rooting for Notre Dame (vs. Deerfield High) and ringing a small cowbell. While Mrs. Ackermann took time out for a brief discussion of suburban hockey, her friend and fellow hockey mother, Mrs. Angela Colasuono, whose son Joe was playing for Notre Dame, made certain the team didn't suffer from lack of vocal support.

Mrs. Ackermann: "I don't care what it costs, it's worth it. It keeps the kids off the streets. . . ."

Mrs. Colasuono: "Atta way, atta way! Come on, you guys, be tough!"

Mrs. Ackermann:" . . . they make new friends, they learn to be aggressive. And they have to do well in school or they won't be out there playing."

Mrs. Colasuono: "Hey, Ref, you subbie!"

(Subbie? "For subnormal," explains Mrs. Colasuono. "One of the nicest things I can call him.")

Mrs. Ackermann: "Hockey's great for

parents too. One thing, you never get ulcers watching a game. You let it all out.''

Mrs. Colasuono: ''Keep the pressure on! Keep shooting! Hey, you're kinda slow with that whistle, aren't you, Ref?''

Whether it's played in Chicago Stadium of the Skokie Skadium, hockey tends to arouse the most feverish instincts of its partisans. If anything, the commitment to hockey may be even more passionate in the hinterlands, where it has, in the last decade, come on with the epidemic force of a flu virus. ''Amateur hockey is the sport of the '70's,'' says Jim Lee, executive director of the Northern Illinois Hockey League. ''Fifteen years ago there was only one indoor rink in the area: now there must be at least 50, with more on the way.'' Lee estimates there are 20,000 boys playing on 1,000 teams all over suburbia, from Lake Forest to Bolingbrook to Flossmoor. Park Ridge alone has 43 teams, with players ranging in age from 7 (Mites) to 19 (Juniors).

There are indications that the new rinks are beginning to ease the severe ice shortage in the Chicago area, where 3 a.m. hockey games have not been unusual. Last year at Carol Stream's Icearena, games were scheduled without letup from 3 o'clock on Friday afternoon until midnight Sunday. But this year, says the rink's assistant manager, Mike Tully, the schedule isn't quite so rugged. There's a breather when no teams are on the ice between 4:30 and 7 a.m. Sundays.

Besides the more obvious benefits it offers young athletes (strong and healthy bodies, lessons in teamwork and sportsmanship, etc.), this suburban hockey crusade could have another important effect, in time: to break the Canadian monopoly on professional hockey. At the moment, for instance, only 24 of the 360 players on National Hockey League rosters are U.S.-born (not one of the 24 is on the Black Hawks). But coaches and parents have high expectations that more than a few of today's amateurs will be tomorrow's pros. Says John Atkinson, a Loop attorney, father of three hockey players, and coach of an Evanston Midget team: ''In 10 years you're going to see a lot of American players on N.H.L. and W.H.A. teams, thanks to programs such as ours.'' Angela Colasuono of Niles agrees: ''When our little Mites get in high school,'' she says, ''they're going to be competition for anybody. And that includes Canadians.''

In the meantime, the amateur hockey leagues, like the pros, will continue to expand and the competition will become even more intense, not just among players but among parents. Most especially among parents, says Bob Murch, who runs the Canadian/American Hockey Group, which helps park districts set up hockey programs (and sells equipment to the players). ''Hockey is a neat activity. There's a place for it, if it's kept in the right perspective, and that's where the trouble comes.

''The Little League syndrome has

taken over. Some parents can't seem to handle the game. They're interested only in having their sons win, because of the personal prestige attached to it. Deep down, there is a crying need for their own ego fulfilment. In some of the — I hate to use these words — less sophisticated communities, you find mothers and fathers wearing jackets with patches showing their sons' exploits and tournaments. In others, they may not wear jackets or emblems, but their emotional involvement is just as strong.''

Such extreme devotion to the sport can occasionally lead to scenes like the one Murch tells of witnessing during a state tournament in Park Ridge a few years ago. "Two mothers were furious; a man had accused one of their sons of being ineligible to play because he was too old, and so they began *spitting* on him. It does get messy at times.''

And away from the ice, Murch says, there's almost as much excitement, though it's not the type that sports writers are accustomed to seeing. "The destiny of community hockey is controled by a closely knit, very powerful group of men. In places like Northbrook and Winnetka, where successful businessmen are involved, the politics of hockey are far more complicated than they are in corporate settings. In Evanston, they recently made the transition from the old guard, which has controlled the key coaching spots, to the new. It was identical to a bloodless coup, and it was very painful to a lot of people.''

But Murch says, "I'm not sure the kids understand the politics of it. They're out there to play, and the issues aren't important to them.''

Despite her family's almost total commitment to hockey, Judy Pigozzi believes they have been able to keep the sport in perspective. "We want our boys to play well and to win. It's fun to win, but we don't want them to take it too seriously. There are things more important — like school. Some of the mothers on Andy's level are particularly intense with their kids, and it puts the wrong kind of pressure on them. As I told one of my sons, 'Use the sport, don't let it use you.' If it stops being fun, what good is it?''

I'M OLDER THAN THE STANLEY CUP

AND I'M STILL SKATING!

BY FRED (CYCLONE) TAYLOR

Last season on network television, I went skating in Vancouver with one of the legendary figures in hockey, Fred (Cyclone) Taylor. The television cameras followed us around the ice in the Pacific Coliseum and we talked about . . . what else? . . . hockey.

Mr. Taylor is 92 years old. I don't know of any 92-year olds who still enjoy skating. Or, for that matter, any 82-year olds or even 72-year olds who still lace on the skates and glide around the ice.

But Cyclone Taylor enjoys it. He even teaches skating . . . to his great grandchildren.

And his mind is just as sharp as the edge on his skates. He recalls vividly great moments from hockey's past, including the team from the Klondike that challenged for the Stanley Cup (see page 14) "It was a great stunt," he says. "But they were a very weak hockey team."

His love for the game shone through as he talked about hockey's early days.

B.M.

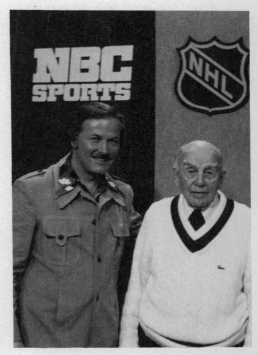

I remember playing hockey with a serious purpose when I was ten years old. Let's see, the Stanley Cup was donated in 1893 so that makes me a few years older than the Cup itself. The young men of that era had just as much desire to play the game as young men do today.

But the people who amazed me were the spectators . . . the fans. They were just as eager to see their team in action as any of the present-day fans. Remember, there were no movies when I was a boy . . . no radios . . . no automobiles. I must pay the highest compliment to the fans at the turn of the century. You can't possibly imagine the hardships they endured . . . the frozen feet . . . the long

Fred (Cyclone) Taylor posed for this photo on somebody's back porch.

138

drives in the horse-drawn sleds ... the blizzards ... the *trials* they went through ... just to see a hockey game.

And often, it wasn't to *see* a game ... it was just to *hear* about a game. Let's say Winnipeg was playing Montreal in a big game ... perhaps a Stanley Cup game. Outside every telegraph office between Winnipeg and Montreal, crowds would gather. They'd stand out in the cold for hours, waiting in their coonskin coats for the local telegrapher to announce through a crack in the frosty window, "Winnipeg scores" or "Montreal scores." That would be all. No details. Just the scores.

Compare those fans with the fans today. If the fan today doesn't like the hockey he sees on television or what he hears on radio, why, he simply turns it off. No more exertion than turning a switch. In the days before radio and television, people walked miles just to hear one hockey score. They couldn't wait to get where they were going.

People remember the players of my day ... and there were some great ones ... and it's an honor for those of us who distinguished ourselves in some small way to be recognized by the Hockey Hall of Fame ... but I like to pay tribute to the fans. Their enthusiasm was remarkable ... something I could never forget.

You ask about my nickname "Cyclone." That was given to me by Malcolm T. Bryce, Sports Editor of the *Ottawa Free Press*. In 1907 they built a new hockey arena in Ottawa and I agreed to play for the Ottawa team.

Our first game was against the famed Montreal Wanderers, Stanley Cup champions the previous year, and the house was packed. Even Lord Grey was there, the Governor General, accompanied by a large party.

I started on a forward line for Ottawa but we soon ran into some difficulty. The problem, it seems, and I hope this doesn't sound immodest, was that my skating was a bit too speedy for my linemates. We simply couldn't click.

Then Petey Green, the trainer of the Ottawa team, suggested a change of strategy.

"Try this young fellow Taylor on defense," he said. Defense, in that era, meant cover point. So they dropped me back and it turned out to be a shrewd move. I scored four goals in that game and the Ottawas skated off with an 8-4 victory. It was a tremendous opening for the home club and the new arena and I was one pleased youngster.

The next day in the *Free Press*, Mr. Bryce wrote: This boy Taylor played a sensational game last night. I understand that when he played for Portage La Prairie he was given the nickname "Tornado" Taylor, and later, when he played in the first pro league in the United States he was called "Thunderbolt" Taylor.

Here and now, I christen this boy "Cyclone" Taylor.

And it stuck. I've been "Cyclone" Taylor ever since.

I'm no longer a "Cyclone" on the ice. But I'm older than the Stanley Cup ... and I'm still skating.

---

*

Jack Ulrich, a player with Victoria shortly after the turn of the century, never argued with opponents or referees and never heard abuse from the fans. Jack Ulrich was deaf and dumb.

Goalie Percy Lesueur used the same goal stick in all league and playoff games for five consecutive years. The stick is now on display in the Hockey Hall of Fame.

WORD QUIZ

```
P  E  L  I  M  E  V  S  C  H  U  L  T  Z  F
E  A  G  L  E  S  O  N  A  C  K  E  T  T  L
T  O  C  T  U  I  Z  D  O  X  K  R  J  T  A
E  H  T  I  M  S  G  E  T  R  E  E  T  Y  M
R  N  G  L  F  L  E  T  A  P  R  I  O  D  E
P  P  R  P  P  I  X  L  L  O  S  T  Q  N  S
U  S  A  T  A  D  C  A  S  H  M  A  N  H  A
C  R  I  B  R  B  U  C  K  S  U  O  C  A  M
K  B  S  Y  E  G  A  Y  O  I  E  U  Q  D  P
M  C  D  N  N  Z  A  E  G  L  O  V  E  R  N
J  E  U  F  T  C  O  R  N  B  I  I  R  O  I
N  P  D  U  N  O  T  I  S  O  P  S  E  F  T
S  F  A  E  L  E  L  P  A  M  D  E  E  L  R
P  I  T  T  S  M  U  M  U  R  O  F  K  U  A
H  O  T  N  O  R  O  T  M  A  H  O  V  P  M
```

Here's an NHL word puzzle. In it are secret words which you find by solving the clues given below. Remember, the words can run in any direction, up, down, across, backwards, or from the bottom. So be careful. The answers can be found in the back of the book.

1. Vancouver Ice Palace
2. Animated announcer
3. Flin Flon Flyer
4. NHLPA President
5. Canuck Crease Minder
6. Boston's Money Man
7. "Soo" Superstar
8. Parry Sound Puckster
9. Mallet Mauler
10. Hab's Legal Eagle
11. Kelly's Heroes
12. Manhatten Cat
13. "Sabre-Sharp" Shooter
14. Brilliant Bernie
15. Ranger Rearguard
16. Dixie "Cup" Team
17. Hall of Fame Home Town
18. West Coast Coach
19. Habitant Hangout
20. Hogtown Center

FRED SHERO

"Freddy Shero? I'll tell you the truth, I don't really know the man. I like him. I respect him, but I don't know him. Maybe his wife does, and his kids, but I don't think anyone will ever be able to figure him out.

"All I know about Freddy Shero is this. He has dedicated his life to this hockey team, and to winning. That's all I have to know."

Bobby Clarke, the captain of the Philadelphia Flyers, was talking about his coach, a man who led the first expansion team to the Stanley Cup in 1974.

Shero, who came to Philadelphia in 1971, is one of the game's great innovators. He was the first coach in the league to admit that he needed a full-time assistant. He now has two, Mike Nykoluk and Barry Ashbee, whose hockey career was ended when a flying puck hit him above the eye.

Shero's philosophy is one of hard work and courage:

"I try to make practice competitive," he says. "Nobody on our team has missed practice in two years, not even guys who are injured. They don't want to miss the laughs. I don't think that you can instruct anyone unless you amuse them first."

But while Shero amuses his team, he also teaches them a pride and dedication to the game which is often found lacking in many of today's professional athletes. The Flyers, or Broad Street Bullies as they've often been designated, play good, tough hockey, They're not afraid to go into the corners for fear of losing their fat wallets:

"There are four corners in a hockey rink and a pit in front of the net," Shero says. "You have to hold your ground. There isn't a man on my team who is afraid to go into the corner and hit someone. Other players on other teams make sure they arrive late. I know guys in this league, superstars in this league, who haven't had a good hit in 10 years."

Shero is an extremely successful motivator. At the start of a season, he hands out what he calls his "bible" to the players. Everybody gets two copies, one for his locker and one for his wallet. If anyone is caught without a copy, he's fined. This "bible" contains the rules of Shero's game, rules he goes over before each game and on which he bases his team's performance in the previous game. This is his formula for winning:

1. Never go off-side on a three-on-two or a two-on one.
2. Never go backwards in your own end except on a power play.

141

3. Never throw a puck out blindly from behind your opponent's net.
4. Never pass diagonally across ice in your own zone unless 100% certain.
5. Wings on wings between blue-lines — except when better able to intercept a stray pass.
6. Second man go all the way for a rebound.
7. Defense with puck at opponent's blue line — look 4 places (other defense, right wing, left wing; center) before shooting.
8. Wing in front of opponent's net must face the puck and lean on stick.
9. Puck carrier over center with no one to pass to and no skating room must shoot it in.
10. No forward must ever turn his back on the puck at any time.
11. No player is allowed to position himself more than two zones away from the puck.
12. Never allow men in your defensive zone to be outnumbered.
13. On a delayed penalty, the puck carrier must look for the extra man at center ice.
14. Be alert to the time left in an opponent's penalty.

Shero's philosophy did not develop out of thin air. He played the game and concentrated on technique. In 1943, Shero was playing hockey when the red line came into effect. Then, coaches emphasized throwing the puck across the line into the other team's zone — in effect, giving it away. Shero's game of controlling the puck in the center zone is practiced by the Flyers, and by the Russians as well. And he got this idea way back in 1943. It still isn't followed by a lot of NHL clubs.

In 1945, while playing for a man named Fred Metcalfe, the idea of the box formation to kill penalties was conceived by Metcalfe. The idea was so successful that people are still trying to figure out a way to get the puck to a man in the box. Shero helped develop the concept, and is now trying to figure out ways to beat it.

These are only two of the many innovations in hockey technique either initiated by Shero or developed by him. Innovations are still taking place in his game. But while Shero is an innovator, he is also a reader. Two books have done a lot, in Shero's opinion, for both the development of the game and Shero's attitude towards it.

"In 1961, I had the happy experience of meeting Antoli Tarasov," recalls Shero, "and since I have read his book maybe fifty times or so. Every time I read it, I understand or learn something new about the game and something I will apply later in my coaching."

Fred Shero also read another book, "They Call Me Coach," by John Wooden, the great basketball coach at U.C.L.A. who retired this year.

"After reading this book, I think the gentleman who wrote it has to be the greatest coach who ever lived in any sport. I have used many of the ideas outlined by him in the past in coaching to help me motivate people, but there is a lot I didn't use and since have incorporated into my philosophy."

So this is a brief look at the philosophy and techniques of Fred Shero. He is in his late 40's now, a former bantam weight boxer in the Navy, a veteran of three National Hockey League seasons as a defenseman with the New York Rangers, another 10 years playing in the minors and 13 more as a minor league coach. He has changed the game, and one wonders why the major leagues took so long to discover him.

HOCKEY FIRST

A couple of years ago Dave Norris of the Toronto Marlies chalked up what must be a hockey "first" when he started a fight in the pre-game warmup. But let's hear how Marlie coach George Armstrong tells the story.

"It all started the night before a game with St. Catharines a couple of years ago," recalls the Chief. "I told my boys at practise they should go home and think how they could help the club. Really concentrate on ways and means of helping the Marlies get going. Apparently Norris gave it a lot more thought than some of the other players. He doesn't get all that much ice time and he figured he'd find a way to take care of the Black Hawks' Wilf Paiement. Paiement, in an earlier game against us, had given us a lot of trouble and scored three goals.

"Now we're in St. Catharines for the game and I'm out having a sandwich when the teams are warming up. Just as the warmup ends and the teams are circling around the ice, skating in opposite direction, Norris decides to make his move. He times his skating until he's almost brushing Paiement every time they pass at center ice. Then, on the last circle, he steps into Paiement and levels him. Paiement jumps up and they have a heck of a fight. Everybody in the place was stunned. And there was nobody around to break it up because the officials were still in their room getting dressed.

"Finally, the referee, Blair Graham, comes running across the ice and he's only wearing his street shoes and a pair of pants. He wades in, slipping and sliding and bare to the waist and pushed the two kids apart. Just in time too, because two other players were starting to throw punches and it might have become a pretty big brawl.

"Graham sent both clubs into the dressing rooms to cool off and that's when I took Norris aside and asked him how it all started. He said, 'Coach, you told us to go home last night and think how we could help the hockey club. That's the best thing I could come with 'cause I don't get on the ice all that much to help in other ways.' Now how can you fault a kid with attitude like that?"

PEE-WEE AND HIS **PALS** by Bill Reid

Taking * Hockey *It's Photos *A * Snap

You see them at every hockey game, big league or minor league. They cluster around the boards during the warmup.

During the game, they lean forward in their seats and focus on the goalmouth action. Game over, they jostle for position in the arena corridor popping flashbulbs as the players clomp off to the dressing room. Who are these people? They're camera buffs ... with one thing in mind. To capture on film their favorite player ... a fight along the boards ... the winning goal.

Their cameras may be cheap or expensive. Aperture openings and shutter speeds may be checked and studied. Film may be color or black-and-white. No matter. Results are often the same ... disappointing.

Why?

Let's meet a professional hockey photographer. He's Robert Shaver of Fort Erie, Ontario. Shaver has been the official team photographer of the Buffalo Sabres for several years and he's an expert at catching hockey action on

"The expression on Jerry Korab's face reflects his displeasure with the referee's call. Hockey is such an emotional game you can often capture reactions ranging from pure delight to pure hatred. One emotion you seldom see in hockey is fear."

6. "Look! Up in the sky. It's a hockey puck! The puck flies high in the air and there's quite a reception committee waiting for it to come down. The photo would have been better if I'd aimed my camera just a shade higher to include the puck but everything happens so quickly in hockey you seldom get perfect shots."

film. For Shaver, taking hockey photos is a snap. For the amateur, it's a challenge that never seems to be mastered.

"In the first place," says Shaver, "taking hockey action photos is not as easy as it looks. Like most things, it's a matter of practice and experience. Then there's a little thing called luck that must be considered.

"A photographer can be changing a roll of film in his camera when the most

145

"It's almost impossible to catch all three members of the French Connection Line in the same photo. They spread out and seldom arrive at the same spot at the same time."

"I like this one because of the expression on the face of Jim Schoenfeld. The man behind the goalie mask is Gary Smith of the Vancouver Canucks."

"You might say 'Up in the Air' describes this shot best. Former Sabre Gerry Meehan goes flying. The only thing touching the ice is the defenseman's left skate."

"Clear the track... here comes Shack. Fast Eddie has done some peculiar things on the ice but climbing up the back of a startled Gerry Ehman took everybody by surprise. I couldn't wait to print the film to see if I'd caught Eddie's antic. I did... and the result was an award-winner."

"When the Islanders first entered the league there was always something going in their net. But Islander Goalie, Glen Resch, was amazed to see Richard Martin wind up there. Some photographers would pass on a shot like this but I found it unusual and interesting.

spectacular play in the game takes place. That's *unlucky*! There's nothing you can do about that. On the other hand you can be ready to shoot, camera loaded, and have the big play take place directly in front of you. That's *luck*!"

Shaver, who has won several awards for his hockey photos, says he likes to follow the players who have "color," men who bring excitement to the game. Gilbert Perrault is a perfect example. Eddie Shack is another. In fact, it was a photo of Shack, taken while he was a Sabre, that earned Shaver international attention and brought him first prize in the annual contest for top hockey photo of the year.

"I like to get as close to the action as possible," says Shaver. "Right up against the glass. That way my camera gets better facial expressions. If you're sitting up in the stands, shooting down, you often get the tops of players' heads and not much more.

"I take a lot of photos during the average game . . . use a lot of film. The more times you click that shutter the better chance you have of capturing a pleasing photo. Using color film can be a little trickier . . . a little more difficult . . . but you can often get good results with color film too."

Robert Shaver does. He's a pro.

For him, hockey photography is easy. It's a snap.

Any Old Patch of Ice Will Do

Someone once estimated that professional hockey players, in preparing themselves for the big leagues, accumulate at least 10,000 hours ice time during their formative years.

This means that pro players, from the time they lace on their first pair of skates until the time they sign their first professional contract, average somewhere between 600 and 1,000 hours ice time *each season* in minor league play and recreational hockey. That's a lot of ice time.

It also means that the player on a team that plays one game a week, and schedules one practice a week, will accumulate only about 50 hours ice time during the season. And remember, during games, *actual* time on the ice is shared with teammates.

So it's rather difficult for a young player who aspires to a professional career to find enough ice time to develop the necessary skills.

That's why many pros come from small communities where any old patch of ice will do.

The young players in the photo reside on a small farm near Grafton, Ontario. Like thousands of other young players, they take advantage of the ice on the nearest frozen pond. Here they practice their shooting, skating and stickhandling and the extra ice time polishes their skills for league games in the community arena.

The extra ice time they devote to hockey is no guarantee they'll be successful hockey players at any level. But it helps.

Ted Lindsay.

Ted Lindsay Says:

"You've Got To Love The Game"

BY BRIAN MCFARLANE

"I've loved this game of hockey ever since I was a little kid," the man said. "I love it now and I'll always love it."

The man is Ted Lindsay, color commentator on televised hockey. As a player, he was there in the glory days of the NHL ... in the late forties and all through the fifties ... when the famed Detroit Production Line of Lindsay, Howe and Abel was discussed the way they discuss the French Connection today. He was there long enough to score 379 goals ... tops among left wingers until a younger man named Bobby Hull passed that total a few years later. He was there 17 years ... long enough to play on nine all star teams ... long enough to help lead the Red Wings to eight league titles (including seven in a row) and four Stanley Cup triumphs.

He was tough ... small but tough. And he played to win. He still plays to win, whether it be with the Detroit Old-timers or a simple game of shinny with some of the boys from the telecast crew.

"It's the only way to play," he emphasizes. "What's the point of playing if you don't play to win. A fellow would have to be awfully strange if he played this game and didn't care whether he won or lost. At least, I'd think him strange ... "

Lindsay can still fly down that left wing. Head up ... graceful ... ice chips flying as he cuts around a floundering defenseman ... a quick fake that pulls the goaltender away from the post ... and clang! ... the rising wrist shot caroms in off the goal post.

"Nice try, goalie," he shouts back over his shoulder, grinning. "But you better learn to guard that post."

The young goalie slams his stick down and growls through his mask. His first words are unintelligible but he ends with something like, " ... get you next time, you lucky old man."

Goalies love to win, too.

Lindsay is almost fifty now but he's in remarkably good shape. Barely an ounce over his playing weight of 168 pounds. Ruggedly handsome. If there's a touch of gray in his thick, black hair only his barber knows it. Fitness experts would do well to employ him as a walking, er ... skating testimonial.

This day, they'd have trouble catching him, unless they're former pros ... because he's on the ice, having fun.

It's a nothing game. Just a bunch of guys from the telecast crew playing another bunch of guys. Tattered sweaters that don't match the stockings. No referee. Casual concern for the rules. Four or five subs at the bench.

I play with Ted ... on the same line. Tim Ryan at center. Without him, Tim and I flounder. With him, we get goals.

Tim Ryan, Lindsay and McFarlane warming up.

It's as simple as that. And scoring goals is always fun.

We're younger but he's faster. And he's in much better shape. We go to the bench and he stays on the ice . . . not even breathing hard . . . happy there are only four subs so he can get a second shift . . . then a third and a fourth. In fact, he's a doggoned sixty-minute man!

Oh, but it's fun to be on his line. Passes click off the blade of your stick, perfectly timed, perfectly placed. You stumble in and take a shot on goal. Heck . . . you didn't mean to shoot it there . . . right at the guy . . . you were aiming for the corner. No matter. Ted barrels in, snaps up the rebound and snaps a shot high into the corner. He laughs, taps the frustrated goalie on the backside and shouts over at me, "Nice play, partner!" Final score: TV Guys 9, Other Guys 7. Two goals late in the game by Lindsay clinch it.

We clump off to the dressing room, exhausted. All but Ted. A young fellow on the other team asks his advice about getting the puck out of the corners. Ted stays out, takes the fellow aside, passes along wisdom accumulated over a lifetime of hockey playing. Nobody will ever say of Lindsay, "I asked the guy a question but he sloughed me off. Too busy, I guess."

Lindsay's never too busy, always willing to spend time with people interested in the game.

Last year, little Hillsdale College in western Michigan needed a hockey coach. Ted's son Blake, a student at the college, phoned home. "Hey, Dad, the guys here want to know if you've got some spare time. We need coaching help."

Ted accepted, on an interim basis, and before long there was a noticeable improvement in the overall play of the Hillsdale team.

"Hockey," he says, "is meant to be played all out. I like the way the Philadelphia Flyers play the game . . .

152

McFarlane tries to avoid a Lindsay check without success.

and the Buffalo Sabres. These teams play with discipline and aggressiveness. They work all the time.

"The Russian players work hard too, and many people say 'Well, the Russians have taken a new approach to hockey.' I don't think the Russians are doing anything new or different. They're just playing the game the way we used to play it."

When Lindsay played the game, in the old six-team NHL, players stuck together. It was something special, something extra special . . . to be a Detroit Red Wing, a Montreal Canadien, a Toronto Maple Leaf.

"We travelled from city to city by train in those days," recalls Ted. "And often two teams would be on the same train. How we hated those guys in the next car! And how we tried to avoid each other. Why, we'd get up an hour early just to get to the dining car and back to avoid meeting those so-and-so's.

"Look at today's players. They play golf together. They work together in hockey schools. They promote hockey equipment for the same company. Players are just too close to their opponents. And the Players' Association has

created one big household for all of them."

But didn't Ted once try to form a players' association himself?

"Yes, I did. Back in the '50's, I helped form an association. I saw it as a vehicle which would be good for the *game* . . . not just the players. If some of the superstars of that era had given our efforts stronger support, our association would have been successful. But most players of that era were frightened to death of management. And the less-talented players were even more afraid. It was a short train ride to the minor leagues for players who rocked the boat.

"Now the pendulum has swung completely in the other direction. It's a players' world today and that's not healthy for the game. I believe the NHL Players' Association has hurt the game. Sure the average player's lot is im-

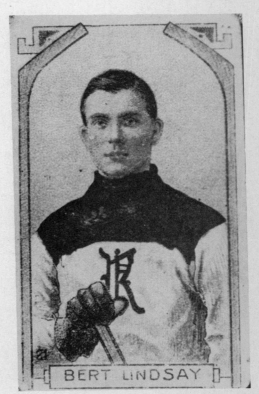

Ted's father, Bert, was a famous hockey player.

153

Lindsay is never too busy to pass along hockey tips to young players. Here he 'intimidates' Barry Blitt into giving up the puck.

proved, improved to the point where complacency sets in and who gets hurt . . . the fan. The guy who pays the shot.

"Players today, even fringe players, get fat long-term contracts. They jump from league to league and find loopholes in their contracts that give them the opportunity to negotiate even richer contracts. And with so much money in the bank, why should players go out and battle in the corners for the puck? Why drop the gloves and risk a punch in the nose? Besides, the guy you're fighting will probably turn out to be the same guy you were palling around with at a summer hockey school just a few weeks earlier.

"No, I think the NHL Players' Association has hurt the game and its founder, Alan Eagleson, is one of the biggest detriments in sport."

Is Eagleson aware of Ted's feelings?

"He should be," is the answer. "I've told him to his face how I feel."

And what was his reaction?

"Well, he sent a letter to each player representative suggesting that the NHL players not co-operate with me in the telecasts of NHL games. But the players, as far as I could determine, just ignored the letter. I get along well with the players and I get the feeling they like me, too."

What about the old-time players, men who feuded with Lindsay on the ice?

Ted laughs. "We meet once in awhile," he says. "On and off the ice. We play against each other in Oldtimers' games and every once in awhile we bristle. We'll hook and hold each other and there'll be the odd scrap. But nothing like the old days."

I recall talking with Rocket Richard at the All Star game in Montreal. Lindsay entered the room and the Rocket said, "There's that Lindsay. Even today, when he walks in the room, I can feel myself get stirred up." I mention this to Ted and he laughs again.

"I interviewed the Rocket that night on television," he says. "And a lot of people expected us to, well, I don't know ... maybe cut each other up or trade insults. But it turned out to be a very warm interview. Very friendly.

"I met some old opponents that night. Stopped by the Montreal table at the All Star Dinner. There was the Rocket ... Toe Blake ... Elmer Lach ... Dickie Moore ... Butch Bouchard. Great players. Good men. We looked each other over ... and I think we all realize we're older now. We fought each other tooth and nail when we played." He says emphatically, drawing out the words "We ... had ... pride. We took pride in playing in a time when only the best played. The seventh best goalie in the world, for example, would be in the minors. Only one goalie to a team. We had pride and we wanted to win. We *all* wanted to win. Nothing else seemed important. And we *loved* the game. There was never any question about that. *We really loved the game.*"

Hockey Heroism

It's not always the forward who scores the big goal, or the goalie who makes the big save, who are the heroes of the hockey teams. On January 5, 1975, the Markham Waxers were playing a game against the Royal York Royals at Chesswood Arena in Downsview, Ontario. Both teams are in the Provincial Junior A league.

During the game the puck was shot into the Markham end, with two players in hot pursuit. The Markham goalie, Eddie Crouch, dived after the puck at the same time. One of the player's skates caught Eddie across the neck, and he went down with a severed carotid artery and partially cut jugular vein.

"When I went down I knew I was cut but I had no idea how bad. I saw the blood spurting, though, and before I could even try to get up, Joe was there," Crouch said.

The "Joe" that Eddie was speaking about is Joe Picininni, Jr., son of a Toronto alderman. Picininni, the trainer of the Waxers, is credited with probably saving Eddie's life with his quick action.

Picininni bolted over the boards to apply direct pressure to the wound and stop the bleeding, which was continued by the ambulance attendants on their way to the hospital.

Dr. Kenneth Richards, Dr. Frank Johnson and Dr. Sol Hyman worked 2½ hours to repair the seven-inch gash in Crouch's neck. The cut reached around the right side of his neck from the middle of his throat.

"I didn't think of the possibility of his dying until much later," Joe said. "I was pretty sure that he would be okay when we got the bleeding controlled."

Bleeding to death was a very distinct possibility, however, for Dr. Richards indicated that Crouch could have bled to death in a matter of a minute.

It is a story with a happy ending. Eddie Crouch rejoined his team on January 18, not to play, but to be presented with an engraved beer stein. Nor was Joe Picininni forgotten. On February 5, he was presented with a civic medal of merit by Mayor David Crombie of Toronto, at a City Hall ceremony.

An accident that could have been a tragedy, except for clear and quick thinking. Eddie's father, a fire chief in Whitby, developed a neck protector for goalies to prevent such accidents, and is presently having it patented. Possibly Mr. Crouch will be a hero in the future if a similar accident can be prevented. All of the hockey heroes aren't on skates.

THE HOCKEY STICK
IT'S ALL A MATTER OF CHOICE

BY GORDIE HOWE
as told to Brian McFarlane

If you ever get to see all the hockey sticks lined up in a big league dressing room you'll notice they differ in length and shape of blade. It's an individual thing . . . all a matter of choice.

When you start out in hockey, sometimes you don't have much choice. I know I didn't. When I was a youngster I used any old stick I could find. I still remember a fellow I idolized giving me one of his old sticks . . . a seven lie . . . and I soon became accustomed to that stick. I liked the stick then and I liked the same type stick later on, in professional hockey. I skated erect, so I could stand a high lie. I also cut the stick off to the point where it was about 50 inches long . . . about five inches less than the maximum allowed. I did this because I liked to carry the puck out in front of me and I wanted to be ready to shoot the puck either right or lefthanded and make plays without wasting any motion.

If your hockey stick is too long, it forces the upper hand in high against your body. The minute that happens you run into all kinds of problems. You have trouble controlling the puck. You lose precious time trying to get the stick into a proper position and you are very apt to look like an awkward little duckling out there.

Jean Beliveau.

156

So it's important to experiment with sticks of different lengths and degree of angle at the blade (lie) until you find one that's just right for you.

There's no written law about the proper length of stick but most hockey men will suggest that young players begin by cutting the shaft of the stick off somewhere between the chin and the nose when it's placed upright against the player's body.

Then, if the puck runs under the blade of the stick close to the heel while a game or practice is underway, the lie of the stick isn't high enough. If it runs under the blade near the toe of the stick, the lie isn't low enough.

It's important to watch other players, study their style of play, and try to determine whether or not they are using the proper stick. Sid Abel, who used to be my centerman in Detroit, liked to hold the puck in close to his skates. He'd use a seven lie stick like myself. And a fellow like Red Kelly, who was with us at the time, would use a four lie stick because he had a tremendous reach and he skated with a bent-over style. Again, it becomes a matter of choice and what's best for you.

From the first time I saw him play, I noticed the great stickhandling ability of my friend Jean Beliveau. He carried the puck out in front of him with both hands, with what seemed like a high lie stick . . . I'd guess between a six and a seven . . . and he led with his chin. By that I mean he skated with his head up, chest out, and it was very difficult to check this man. By carrying the puck in front of him like that, he was able to backhand or forehand the puck and he could play that puck perfectly to either wing. It was just one of the remarkable traits that helped make him what he was . . . one of the greatest centers in the world.

HOW MUCH DO YOU KNOW ABOUT EQUIPMENT?

1. In the NHL, a hockey stick must not be longer than

    a. 50 inches
    b. 55 inches
    c. three feet
    d. the string on your yo-yo

2. The goalie's pads must not be wider than

    a. fifteen inches
    b. seven inches
    c. ten inches
    d. a yard

3. The ordinary hockey puck measures

    a. one inch thick by three inches in diameter
    b. two inches thick by four inches in diameter
    c. three inches thick by five inches in diameter
    d. a foot thick and a foot in diameter

4. The skates the players and officials wear must be equipped with

    a. pink or blue laces
    b. approved safety tips on the heel of the blades
    c. scuff marks
    d. double runners

(Answers at the back of the book)

Santa Skates and Scores!

Does Santa Claus skate and play hockey? Of course he does. There's plenty of ice at the North Pole and Santa often finds time to slip on an old pair of skates, take his hockey stick and practice his shooting and his stickhandling.

"I could stand to lose a little weight," he laughs. "Sometimes, when the puck is down around my feet I lose sight of it. But I still love to play the game."

Santa's skills on ice were quite evident during a recent visit to the Montreal Forum. He warmed up slowly, then dashed around the ice with the speed of a Cournoyer and the grace of a Lafleur.

To amuse a small number of onlookers (in the manner of Pete Mahovlich) he turned the blade of his stick over and speared the puck on its flat surface . . . propelling it this way and that, twisting his body to avoid imaginary checkers . . . and not once did the puck get away from him.

This little manoeuvre had rinksiders applauding.

Then, with a flourish and a quick flip of the wrists, he drilled the puck expertly . . . high into an empty net. Orr . . . Esposito . . . Martin . . . Dionne . . . none could have done it better.

Then, like all great scorers . . . Santa raised his arms high in the familiar gesture that signals GOAL!

Answers to Quizzes

Photo Quiz on page 23

1. Mark Howe
2. Jim Rutherford
3. Jean Potvin
4. Danny Grant
5. Pete LoPresti
6. Henry Boucha

True Or False Quiz on page 49

1. True
2. True
3. False. Keon has always been a Leaf.
4. False. Punch never made it to the NHL.
5. True
6. True
7. True
8. True
9. True
10. True

Word Puzzle on page 79

1. Perrault
2. Maki
3. Cournoyer
4. Ververgaert
5. Broda
6. Howe
7. Blake
8. Worsley
9. Orr
10. Beliveau
11. Marson
12. Polis
13. Keon
14. Meehan
15. Savard
16. Parent
17. Resch
18. Toronto
19. Kelly
20. Plante
21. Leach
22. Richard

Hockey Quiz on page 102

1. 1
2. 1
3. 3
4. 1
5. 3
6. 2
7. 3
8. 1
9. 3
10. 2

Hockey Quiz on page 157

1.b   2.c   3.a   4.b

Hockey Nicknames on page 122

1.— 9.	15.—14.	28.—23.
2.— 7.	16.— 6.	29.—35.
3.— 2.	17.—11.	30.—28.
4.—15.	18.—12.	31.—24.
5.—19.	19.—16.	32.—40.
6.—13.	20.—10.	33.—26.
7.— 4.	21.—39.	34.—30.
8.—17.	22.—31.	35.—27.
9.— 1.	23.—21.	36.—29.
10.—20.	24.—34.	37.—38.
11.— 8.	25.—22.	38.—32.
12.— 3.	26.—37.	39.—36.
13.—18.	27.—25.	40.—33.
14.— 5.		

Hockey quiz on page 129

A-3, The penalty timekeeper must tell the player how much time remains in the penalty if he is asked. B-2, C-2, D-2, E-1.

Word Puzzle on page 140

1. Pacific Coliseum
2. Peter Puck
3. Clarke
4. Eagleson
5. Smith
6. Cashman
7. Esposito
8. Orr
9. Schultz
10. Dryden
11. Maple Leafs
12. Emile
13. Martin
14. Parent
15. Park
16. Flames
17. Toronto
18. Pulford
19. Forum
20. Keon